W9-BGF-930

Growing Up in The People's Republic

Palgrave Studies in Oral History

Series Editors: Linda Shopes and Bruce M. Stave

Growing Up in The People's Republic

Conversations between Two Daughters of China's Revolution

Ye Weili

with

Ma Xiaodong

GROWING UP IN THE PEOPLE'S REPUBLIC
© Ye Weili with Ma Xiaodong 2005.

All rights reserved. No part of this book may be used or reproduced in any manner whatsoever without written permission except in the case of brief quotations embodied in critical articles or reviews.

First published in 2005 by
PALGRAVE MACMILLAN™
175 Fifth Avenue, New York, N.Y. 10010 and
Houndmills, Basingstoke, Hampshire, England RG21 6XS
Companies and representatives throughout the world.

PALGRAVE MACMILLAN is the global academic imprint of the Palgrave Macmillan division of St. Martin's Press, LLC and of Palgrave Macmillan Ltd. Macmillan® is a registered trademark in the United States, United Kingdom and other countries. Palgrave is a registered trademark in the European Union and other countries.

ISBN 1–4039–6995–7
ISBN 1–4039–6996–5 (pbk.)

Library of Congress Cataloging-in-Publication Data

Ye Weili.
    Growing up in the People's Republic : conversations between two daughters of China's revolution / by Ye Weili with Ma Xiaodong.
        p. cm.—(Palgrave studies in oral history)
        ISBN 1–4039–6995–7—ISBN 1–4039–6996–5 (pbk.)
        1. China—History—Cultural Revolution, 1966–1976—Personal narratives. 2. Ye Weili. 3. Ma Xiaodong. I. Title: Conversations between two daughters of China's revolution. II. Ma Xiaodong. III. Title. IV. Series.

DS778.7.W445 2005
951.05'6—dc22   2005048676

A catalogue record for this book is available from the British Library.

Design by Newgen Imaging Systems (P) Ltd., Chennai, India.

First edition: December 2005

10 9 8 7 6 5 4 3 2 1

Transferred to digital printing in 2006

To my mother Bai Tian and my father Fang Shi, whose path is my legacy; to my son Yuanyuan, may mine be his.

Ya Weili's picture taken in the Summer of 2004, at Cape Cod, MA.

Ma Xiaodong's picture taken in December 2002 at a conference in Shanghai.

Contents

Series Editors' Foreword

China, despite the nation's current preoccupation with the Middle East, is perpetually on the American mind. Many observers believe that the twenty-first century will be the Chinese Century as that country industrializes and modernizes. From a historical perspective, China in the twentieth century was among the most tumultuous nations in the world. Ye Weili's study primarily deals with a particular decade of tumult, chaos, and political warfare, 1966–1976, the Great Proletarian Cultural Revolution, but explores experience before and after as well. It does so from the perspective of two women, Professor Ye and Ma Xiaodong, who tell their stories of life during the Cultural Revolution in dialogue with each other. The two voices, obtained through tape recorded conversations conducted originally in Chinese and then translated into English, add a special and complex dimension to the existing genre of individual memoirs of the period. The book is unusual in its departure from the frequent victimization approach to the Cultural Revolution as Ye Weili and Ma Xiaodong discuss the texture and continuity of everyday life in the midst of turbulent change. In this, and in its gendered approach to the period, the book makes a special contribution. It reflects oral history's ability to humanize events and articulate the drama of an era. It also attempts to knit together oral history and memoirist writing.

In so doing, it offers an example of the capacity of oral history to capture the memory of the past and allows us to understand the past from the perspective of the present. Joining with Ye Weili and Ma Xiaodong in their effort to sort out the puzzle of their generation—why it became so caught up in the Cultural Revolution and involved in violence—the reader travels a path of adventure, excitement, and, most significantly, introspection. The journey may make China more understandable or, perhaps, raises new questions about its development.

Whichever, this addition to the Palgrave Studies in Oral History series helps broaden its geographic base by introducing a study of a major Asian nation. The series serves as a big tent not simply geographically, but methodologically as well.

In this instance, unlike the typical process, the oral historian is the subject of the oral history. Ordinarily, the interviewer helps shape someone else's story. By recording her dialogue with Ma Xiaodong, Ye Weili demonstrates the truly conversational aspect of oral history. It is through discussion between the two principals that the narrative is developed and that the point–counterpoint of their varied experience is clarified. The series welcomes new approaches under the big tent and looks forward to future innovations in oral history.

Bruce M. Stave
University of Connecticut

Linda Shopes
Pennsylvania Historical Museum Commission

Foreword

This highly unusual memoir recounts what it was like for Ye Weili and her collaborator Ma Xiaodong to experience girlhood, adolescence, and early adulthood in China in the years leading up to and then embracing the Cultural Revolution (1966–1976). The memoir is unique in a number of important respects. For one thing, it raises unsettling questions concerning the highly simplified and unrelievedly negative picture that we often get of the latter decades of the Mao era. This negative image was fostered partly by such developments as the end of the cold war and the triumph of global capitalism, partly by the "victim" literature written by people who experienced the later Mao years personally and then came to the West and detailed their sufferings in published accounts. Ye and Ma don't deny the grizzlier aspects of the Cultural Revolution decade—indeed, a particularly horrific incident that took place at Ye's school in Beijing forms an important part of the story. But when, many years later, they began a series of conversations about their experiences they both sensed that, in the starkly downbeat depiction of this period that has gained general currency in the West, there was no place for them to fit memories that were dear to them, making it extremely difficult to reconstruct their individual growing-up experiences in a more complex, honest, and balanced way.

Many of the accounts of this period, for example, focus on large-scale sociopolitical phenomena (violent campaigns, societal breakdown, Red Guard rampaging, and the mass performances of Chairman Mao in Tiananmen Square) and tend in the process to pay little attention to what Ye refers to as "the texture of everyday life," the "multiple shades of gray in a huge society." In the memoir a special effort is made to incorporate such details, in implicit defiance of the political ethos of the day. When we hear about what dinner table conversations were like, family domestic helpers, Ye's and Ma's parents' relationships with one another, their reactions to seeing their fathers cry for the first time, and the games they played as children, we are furnished with important contextual material for the bigger, external happenings that loomed so large in young people's lives at the time.

A second way in which the memoir is distinctive is the manner in which it is structured. Substantial portions of the text are framed not as a single-person narrative but as a conversation between Ye and Ma, in which they ask questions of each other and compare notes on aspects of their shared past. I know of no other account of these turbulent years that is presented in this way. Aside from its high readability, the conversational approach has two very important virtues. First, it makes clear that, although at a certain level of generality, Ye's and Ma's experiences were indeed parallel—both were females who grew up in Beijing at the same time, joined the Red Guards, worked in rural areas starting in the late 1960s, and went overseas to study in the post–Mao years—when one peers beneath the radar screen and looks more closely, one discovers how utterly different and distinctive individual life experiences could be. Ye's father was very liberal, encouraged his children to have independent ideas, and tolerated lively disagreement at family meals, while Ma's father was stricter and more patriarchal. Although many Red Guard groups were rigidly ideological and dogmatic in conduct, when Ma had to leave her group after her mother was beaten and given a "devil's hair-cut," her classmates in the group, instead of shunning her, made it clear that they were sorry she could no longer be one of them. In the late 1960s, when "educated youth" (*zhiqing*) like Ye and Ma were sent to the countryside, Ma's experience on a state farm in Yunnan and Ye's experience living and working in a village in northern Shanxi turned out to be poles apart.

The other thing that the conversational structuring of mush of the memoir clearly brings out is the salience of individual personality. The ways in which Ye and Ma responded to their experiences, even the broadly similar ones, were far from identical. As the tempo of revolutionary fervor increased dramatically at the onset of the Cultural Revolution, Ye consistently experienced difficulty thinking and feeling as she was supposed to. She held back and resisted throwing herself into the political movements swirling about her, desperately trying to preserve some sense of separateness and self. Ma, responding very differently, quickly (and, it appears, happily) surrendered to the new revolutionary culture. She wanted to be a hero, a soldier, and reacted strongly against the stereotyped female behavior encountered in books, where women giggled instead of laughing heartily. She too wanted to laugh heartily, like men.

The different personal make-ups of the two women come across with equal vividness in their accounts of their subsequent experiences in the countryside. Inspired by the "iron girl" (*tie guniang*) model, Ma, on her state farm in Yunnan, was intent on being the equal in all things of her male counterparts, even going so far as to conceal her monthly periods so that she wouldn't have to take the customary day or two off from work and fall behind. Yet, in her appreciation of the beauty of her physical surroundings, the tentative awakening of romantic feeling that she briefly experienced, and the close friendships she made with other young women in her group, Ma during these years also revealed a less politically correct side of her personality. Ye's experience in rural Shanxi was much less regimented than Ma's. Characteristically, she liked the idea of being sent to a village, since anybody could be a peasant and she didn't have to deal with political screening. Also characteristically, in a good part of her account, Ye presents herself as an outside observer, noting the extreme poverty of this part of the country, the freer sexual mores of the villagers, their relative indifference (as compared to city people) to political rectitude, and so on. In some respects, Ye casts herself as an outsider even in regard to the rest of the *zhiqing* cohort in the village. (Admittedly naïve and puritanical at the time, she is shocked to learn that members of the group were also, like the villagers, engaging in premarital sex.) For most of her five years in the countryside, Ye did agricultural work, initially enjoying it but eventually finding the repetitiveness of farming stultifying and wondering whether this was all there was going to be to her life.

Ye and Ma both left the countryside in 1973 and attended college of several years as "worker–peasant–soldier" students. This was the final phase of the Cultural Revolution. Politics took precedence over academic learning and there was a good deal of tension on campuses. Ye found her college experience depressing. She hated the regimentation of school life, which formed a sharp contrast to the freedom she had enjoyed in her village, and felt that she had to live a lie in order to survive. Ma (like Ye) experienced the tension rife at the time between students of peasant and urban backgrounds, the former being less well educated but far more powerful politically. But she was less bothered than Ye by the regimentation. The reader is not surprised to learn that Ma, ever the enthusiastic joiner, eventually became a member of the Communist Party, while Ye displayed no interest in following this path.

The variety of individual experience and personality elicited by the conversational strategy adopted in this memoir challenges in a powerful way the drab picture of complete conformity often understood to have characterized the last years of the Maoist era. By the time we have laid the book down, we have a strong sense of the individuality of its two contributors, how very different they were as human beings.

One other special strength of the memoir is its fascinating evocation of the difference between immediate experience and subsequent reflection on that experience. Again and again, for instance, the point is made that when Ye and Ma were youngsters in China they lacked a "gendered" sensibility. In adulthood, however, both of them learned to appreciate gender as an important component of identity, with the consequence that their memories of their growing-up experiences as young women were reshaped. This struck me, when I read the memoir, as a marvellous example of how the "experienced" past, which is initially framed by one context, becomes reframed when individuals look back on their earlier lives and, operating as "historians," reformulate them from the vantage point of what they have learned since. "Remembering," for Ye and Ma, far from being a simple matter of repossession of the past, becomes a process governed by new frames of reference that the two women were not cognizant of in their youth, with the result that, on the level of consciousness, the past retrieved is very different from the past as originally experienced.

The difference in perspective derived from radical spatial relocation also needs to be factored in here. Ye says that the years living in the countryside enabled her and many others in her generation to reconnect with the humanistic values of their childhood years (in the 1950s and early 1960s), which in turn positioned them intellectually and emotionally to embrace the new world that opened up in the post–Mao era. Living abroad later on—Ye and Ma both left China in the 1980s for further study in the United States—also provided for both women important new vantage points from which to look back on and reformulate the experiences of their childhood and adolescence.

Many of the best-known personal accounts of the later Mao years—I have in mind such books as Gao Yuan's *Born Red* (1987), Yue Daiyun's *To the Storm* (1985), and Liang Heng's *Son of the Revolution* (1983)—were written within a relatively short time following Mao's death in 1976. One of the great strengths of Ye Weili's memoir, in contrast to these earlier works, is precisely its distance from the events and experiences recounted. This distance, spatial as well as temporal, enables the author and her collaborator to reflect on their experiences in distinctive ways and to raise issues that the earlier accounts were unable, or at least less able, to broach. The result is a probing, courageously honest, and enormously insightful piece of writing, the appeal of which should extend well beyond the world of China specialists. It will make compelling reading for psychologists who study memory, students of gender, and historians of childhood. Written in engaging and lively prose, with an abundance of personal (often unusually intimate) detail, it should also be of great interest to the general reader.

Paul A. Cohen

Explanation of Chinese Names

Throughout the book the names for Chinese people appear in the order of family name first and given name second, according to the Chinese way. All the names are in *pinyin*.

Chronology of Major Events in China: 1949–Present

Date	History
1949	Founding of the People's Republic of China (PRC).

1950–1953   Korean War (domestically the Resist-America-Aid-Korea campaign was launched).

Land Reform (redistribution of land and classification of rural population / accompanied with class struggle and continued from prior to the founding of the PRC).

Marriage law (granting people the right to choose marriage partners / wives the right to initiate divorce / women the right to inherit property / abolishing concubinage and marriage for sale).

1951   Suppressing counterrevolutionaries campaign (targeting those with Nationalist connections).

Three Anti-campaign (aiming at corruption, waste, and obstructionist bureaucracy / targeting Chinese Communist Party (CCP) cadres).

1952   Five Anti-campaign (aiming at tax evasion and other wrong-doings / targeting private business owners.

1953   The first Five-Year Plan (based on Soviet model / achieving a dramatic increase in industrial production).

1953–1956   Rural Collectivization.

1955   Denounciation of Hu Feng, a prominent writer, for alleged counterrevolutionary thinking and activities. Thousands of people were affected and persecuted.

1956   The eighth CCP conference / Liu Shaoqi announced in the keynote speech that the period of intense class struggle was over and the focus of the country now was on economic development; references to the importance of Mao Zedong Thought were dropped, reflecting possibly the influence of the Twentieth Congress of the Soviet Communist Party at which Khrushchev criticized Stalin's personality cult.

1956–1957   Nationalization and collectivization of private business in urban China; celebration of China entering the "socialist stage."

The "Hundred Flowers" period—following the Twentieth Congress of the Soviet Communist Party, the CCP leadership initially encouraged a more open and freer society in China by "letting a hundred flowers bloom and a hundred schools of thought contend."

1957   Anti-rightist campaign. Those who spoke up to criticize party and government policies were caught and labeled anti-party "rightists."

1958   The Great Leap Forward (GLF); launched initially to speed up economic development through mass mobilization; large-scale collectives called "communes" were established in rural areas. Many peasant women participated in agricultural work for the first time in their lives. Dining halls were set up to replace private kitchens. Ambitious public works and projects drew away large number of able-bodied male laborers from agricultural work. Production figures were often greatly exaggerated by local cadres to impress superiors.

1959   At a party conference held at Lushan, Jiangxi province, Peng Dehuai, Minister of Defense, criticized Mao's GLF policies. He was dismissed from his post.

1960   Soviet Union withdrew technicians from China. Sino-Soviet rift became public.

1959–1961   "Three years of natural disaster"—the official explanation for the widespread material hardship in the country. While urban China faced a serious shortage of food supply, rural China was caught in one of the worst famines in history and suffered an incredibly high death toll.

Pragmatic leaders such as Liu Shaoqi, Zhou Enlai, and Deng Xiaoping followed a policy of economic retrenchment to fix problems caused by the GLF.

On the cultural front there was a more relaxed atmosphere, which led to appearance of literary, film, and drama products that would later be criticized as "poisonous weeds."

Mao Zedong, meanwhile, retired from the "front line," releasing himself from much of the day-to-day business of state affairs. He gave Liu Shaoqi the post of head of the state.

1962   "Seven thousand people" party conference was convened at the beginning of the year—an important meeting to examine the problems of the GLF with an open-mind. Liu Shaoqi contended that the vast majority of the errors had been caused by men rather than "nature." Mao made a reluctant self-criticism.

Riots occurred at the Sino-Soviet border in Xinjiang; a border war was fought between China and India in the fall; the Nationalist government in Taiwan intensified their efforts to "retake" the mainland.

At the tenth plenum of the eighth party conference, the tone was changed dramatically from earlier in the year. It was set by Mao in his harsh "never forget class struggle" speech. To him the class struggle situation was severe both at home and abroad. This basic assessment became the backdrop for what to come in the following years.

1963   The Sino-Soviet ideological conflict accelerated. The first of a series of nine articles denouncing "revisionism" of the Soviet appeared in *The People's Daily*.

Quotations from Chairman Mao (Mao's little red book) were studied first by the People's Liberation Army (PLA) and then by the rest of the country as a sort of "red Bible," pushing Mao's personality cult to an unprecedented new height. Lin Biao, the head the PLA, became a political super star.

"The socialist education campaign" was launched, under which class struggle was reemphasized; in rural China it was conducted in the form of "four cleanups" campaign.

1964–1965   The socialist education campaign continued and intensified across the land in various forms, such as the "revolutionizing movement" taking place in secondary schools in Beijing.

1966   Launching the Cultural Revolution.

1968	The height of "up to the mountains down to the countryside" movement. Millions of urban youth were sent down to rural China.
1969	The nineth CCP conference. Lin Biao's position as Mao's successor was written into the party's constitution.
1971	On September 13 an airplane carrying Lin Biao and his family crashed in Outer Mongolia. Allegedly Lin had tried to assassinate Mao. When the plot failed, Lin tried to flee to the Soviet Union only to be killed in the plane crash.
	The Lin Biao Incident took the entire country by surprise. Many people began to wonder in private about the justification of the Cultural Revolution. Disillusionment became widespread.
1972	U.S. president Richard Nixon visited China.
1973	Deng Xiaoping, fallen earlier as the no.2 target of the Cultural Revolution, returned to Beijing to assist Zhou Enlai to bring some order to the economy and other areas badly affected by the Cultural Revolution.
1974–1975	Heated struggle between radical Cultural Revolution leaders represented by Mao's wife Jiang Qing and moderate leaders such as Zhou and Deng. A series of political campaigns were launched by the radical leaders to attack the moderate leaders. Mao was behind the campaigns and his heart was with the radicals, but he managed to keep certain balance between the two factions.
1976	Zhou Enlai died in January.
	In the spring urban residents across the land mourned the death of Zhou; the activities soon turned political and amounted to a popular protest movement against the Cultural Revolution. It was quickly suppressed. Deng Xiaoping was accused of being the "black hand" behind the scene and was purged again.
	Mao died in September.
	Within a month of Mao's death Jiang Qing and three other radical leaders, nicknamed the "Gang of Four," were arrested. The Cultural Revolution finally came to an end.

1978	The third plenum of the eleventh CCP conference, held at the end of the year, marked a most significant change in the CCP policy. Rhetoric on class struggle was dropped. Economic development now became the goal of the country and "modernization" the catchword.
	Posters written by ordinary citizens appeared on a stretch of wall in downtown Beijing to reflect upon the lessons of the Cultural Revolution. Political reform was raised as imperative to prevent another Cultural Revolution from happening again. Called "the democracy wall movement," it was eventually put down.
1980s	A dynamic decade that witnessed profound changes in the country's economic, social, and cultural life. Sending students to study abroad to seek modern knowledge became a national policy.
	Political reform remained largely handicapped, yet there were signs that space was being pushed open slowly for a politically more tolerant society.
	A series of political campaigns were launched by the conservatives within the party to counter "spiritual pollution" and "bourgeois liberalization." These campaigns failed to produce the same harsh effects as those in the previous decades.
	High inflation, widely spread corruption, along with other problems resulted from rapid transformation of the society led to a high degree of social strains.
1989	Triggered by the death of Hu Yaobang, a popular CCP leader forced to resign a few years earlier, a protest movement was started by college students in Beijing to demand a more open and fair society. It soon drew support from the rest of the urban populace. Significantly, freedom of press was called upon by the demonstrators.
	Neither the government nor the students were able to find a middle ground to negotiate a common agreement. The protest movement was finally put down with military force by the hardliners in the government on June 4. Hundreds of people were killed.
1990s	The decade witnessed rapid economic growth, especially along the coastal regions, after an initial set-back in the wake of "June 4th." To become rich was not only allowed but glorified.

A huge gap quickly emerged to separate a small number of new rich (some were super rich) from a sizable number of people who failed to benefit from the economic boom, many living either in remote interior, rural areas or in abandoned factory towns—China's equivalent for "rust belt." Widespread corruption plagued the entire country.

People in general found a larger space in their daily, private lives.

Meanwhile, political reform fell way behind economic development.

2000–Present   China entered the new century with continuous fast-pace economic growth on the one hand and many urgent challenges in political, social, and environmental realms on the other hand.

Acknowledgments

Writing this book has meant many things to me: it has helped me sort out the complicated legacy of the era in which I lived my youth. It has connected me with both my parents' and grandparents' generations. It has also helped heal me from a series of personal losses in the last decade. The process of working on this book has uplifted me, sustained me, and ultimately helped me become a stronger, more sensible, and more understanding human being.

During this long course I have encountered enormous kindness, encouragement, intellectual help, and moral support. My first and foremost thanks go to Ma Xiaodong, my conversational partner and good friend. Without her graciously sharing her story, this book would be much less interesting. I also want to thank Lin Chun for her initial participation in the project. For over a year the three of us had many memorable intellectual exchanges and a great deal of pure fun.

Some of the most highly respected scholars in the field of Chinese studies have helped shape the manuscript at its various stages. I owe my hugest intellectual debt to Paul Cohen, who not only has given me big-hearted support along the way but also written a most kind foreword to endrose the book. I am very grateful to Chris Gilmartin, Gail Hershatter, John Israel, Steve Levine, Ezra Vogel, Carolyn Wakeman, and Marilyn Young for their astute comments and generous encouragement. Chris and Marilyn, in particular, have cared for the author and her project in more ways than one. I am very thankful to Lynn Struve, who invited me to present a section of the manuscript at the Memory Link workshop at Indiana University in Bloomington in the fall of 2003, at which David Pillemer, a highly regarded scholar on memory studies, offered expert critiques; and to Vera Shwarcz, who elevated a key chapter with her magic poetic touch and backed the project at a critical point.

My special thanks also go to Catherine Manton, a friend and former colleague, who made invaluable contributions to the book by strengthening the prose and turning it into a much more colloquial form of writing. The many days of working with Cathy in her Cape Cod home, sitting across the dinner table and reading aloud the parts of Ye and Ma (to hear if they *sounded* right) has remained in my mind the most enjoyable moments in the production of the book.

Other friends at University of Massachusetts Boston have offered bountiful collegial support and intellectual help. To Ann Cordilia, Kate Hartford, Jean Humez, Winston Langley, Esther Kingston-Mann, and Lois Rudnick I owe great professional and personal debts. Jean Humez in particular has stood by my side throughout these years as a most trustworthy colleague and a caring mentor.

So many other people have offered their support and help that I cannot possibly thank everyone. I would, however, like to single out a few here: John Canty, Kathy Klyce, Sara Walden, Anne and John Watts. I would also like to use this opportunity to express my long-overdue gratitude to Joan Afferica, a history professor at Smith College whom I have regarded as a mentor ever since I first arrived in the United States years ago. It is only fitting that her suggestions on the last paragraphs of my section put a nice, final touch to my story. Big thanks also go to Zhu Hong, who has helped sharpen both the ideas and the wording of the book with her shrewd comments and superb mastery of the English language. I owe a special debt to Peter Gilmartin, who kind-heartedly organized a small group of enthusiastic high school English teachers to read and critique the manuscript at a time when I badly needed feedbacks and assurance.

A number of my students and a few other college-aged young people have read sections of the manuscript and offered their comments. I want to thank them for their shrewd observations and encouraging remarks.

My two editors at the Palgrave Studies in Oral History series, Bruce Stave and Linda Shopes, have given me so much more support and help than any author can hope for from her editor. I owe them a heart-felt "Thank you!"

I am also extremely grateful to my school, University of Massachusetts, Boston, which has provided financial support at three different points to enable me to pursue this project to its completion.

My final thanks must go to my Chinese friends who have read and commented on the project (the Chinese version): Yu Ling, Li Ruolin, Feng Jinglan, Liu Xinru, Li Heping, Luo Ning, Song Shaopeng, Liang Xiaoyan, and Zheng Yefu—some are here in the United States, others are in China. To this long list I also want to add Carma Hinton, a China-born American. Most of these people are my peers who shared similar growing-up experience in the Mao era as mine. Their critiques have special meaning to me and are particularly valued.

Introduction

Personal Quest and Global Milieu

I instantly connected with Ma Xiaodong when we first met in Boston. It was a decade ago when she was a graduate student in sociology and I taught history at a local university. It delighted me to find a fellow Beijinger, but more than the common birthplace, it was the parallel experience of our youth in China that made me feel an immediate affinity for her.

At the time I felt a strong urge to look back, if only because at middle age I had a need to know where I came from. This existential craving was compounded by my anxiety about the meaning of my earlier life. With the end of the cold war and the subsequent ascendancy of global capitalism, much of my experience growing up in the first decades of the People's Republic of China (PRC), often referred to as the Mao (Zedong) era, seemed to be invalidated by the triumph of the capitalist West. Publication of many Chinese memoirs in the West, mostly written by victims of various political campaigns during the Mao years, reinforced a prevailing negative image of this period.[1] Some of these works were enormously successful and thus became a kind of yardstick against which the lives of other Chinese would be measured and judged.

I felt the pressure to measure up. The attempts, however, led to my bewilderment. I empathized with those memoirists who had suffered greatly from political purges in the Mao era, as some of my close relatives had been caught in a similar predicament. But I also realized that, when measured by their yardstick, significant segments of my own life experience vanished, memories dear to my heart found no place to fit, and I was at a loss to explain who I was.

I told Ma Xiaodong about my confusion. She shared my feelings. When I invited her to be my conversational partner in an oral history project to jointly trace our youthful years in China, she readily agreed. Further conversation made us realize that we had another reason for this collaborative inquiry. As youngsters we both lacked an awareness of gender. Now with more life experience, greater maturity, and exposure to Western feminism, we had learned to appreciate gender as an important component of identity. We decided to reassess, through this acquired gendered lens, our growing-up female experience in a period when many radical changes occurred in Chinese women's lives.

During the years of 1994 and 1995, we met regularly on weekends, alternating meeting places between our homes. With a tape recorder on the table, we acted as each other's interviewer, commentator, occasional inquisitor, and, of course, audience. We decided to begin with our early childhood and end with the 1980s when each of us came to the United States. By making a thorough inventory, so to speak, of our individual life experiences in China with someone who had lived through the same time, we hoped to check the reliability of our memories, to sort out a time period that had both nurtured and indoctrinated us, and ultimately to make some sense out of our prior lives in China.

A Generational Angle / A Disturbing Puzzle

In many ways our stories can be read as two case studies about the making of a distinct generation in recent Chinese history. Born around 1950, our generation coincided with American baby boomers. The life course of this generation paralleled the trajectory of the newly founded PRC. While individual situations might vary, significant similarities existed in the way people in this age cohort were raised, thanks largely to the uniformity of education we received since childhood. This was especially true for those living in urban areas.

Ultimately it was the Cultural Revolution (1966–1976) that created our generation. We entered adolescence and young adulthood, an especially impressionable stage in people's lives, at precisely the time when political *and* social order was turned upside down and the entire country was swept into a turmoil almost overnight. Both as individuals and as a group, we underwent some of the most severe trials and tribulations possible in life. It was this shared destiny of our youth that forged a strong generational bond among us, explaining why Ma Xiaodong and I quickly hit it off when we first met.

At the beginning of the Cultural Revolution in the summer of 1966, many people in our age group eagerly responded to Chairman Mao's call, "It's right to rebel," acting as the vanguard in the great leader's grandiose scheme to smash the Old World. Both Ma Xiaodong and I encountered violence in an unforgettable way. In my school female students beat a school leader to death. Ma Xiaodong participated in beating an alleged class enemy on her school campus, only to find a few days later that her own mother, leader of a secondary school, suffered severe physical abuse at the hands of her students. Violence was pervasive at this stage of the Cultural Revolution, frequently committed by teenage students who called themselves Red Guards.

In today's China the Cultural Revolution is still a sensitive topic, especially when it comes to the subject of violence. There is a general silence on the part of former Red Guards to talk about that detestable phase in their youth.[2] No former students in my school, for instance, have openly admitted taking part in the beating of our school leader. The dead woman's husband, a frail old man now in his eighties, is still waiting for an apology almost 40 years later.[3]

My school was one of the finest secondary girls' schools in Beijing before the Cultural Revolution. How could a group of nice girls turn into murderers so quickly, when only a few months earlier everything still appeared normal in the school? How were members of my generation capable of behaving in such a ferocious manner? These questions haunted me for years. They were in the back of my mind when I invited Ma Xiaodong to join me in examining our earlier lives. To a certain extent this oral history reflects our collective effort to solve the puzzles about our generation.

People have offered various explanations.[4] Some have argued that students' education since the 1949 revolution was responsible. Growing in a cultural wasteland that insulated them from humanist traditions on the one hand, and indoctrinated with class-struggle rhetoric on the other, it was no wonder that youngsters would behave the way they did once unleashed by the Cultural Revolution. It has been said that this generation was fed on "wolves' milk." What behavior would you expect from young wolves?

In her influential study of a group of former Red Guards, Anita Chan makes a scholarly yet similar assessment of the Chinese educational system, arguing that the system induced an "authoritarian personality" that would manifest in students' violent behavior at the start of the Cultural Revolution.[5] It is noteworthy that Chan emphasizes the *consistency* of authoritarianism in students' experience since the 1950s.

Ma Xiaodong and I do not think this categorical depiction fit our reality well. We did not attend many political sessions at the elementary level as Chan reports. Our lives during that period consisted of many normal childhood activities. Ma Xiaodong remembers how she was encouraged to develop her talent in athletics. A fond memory I have was an event at the picturesque Beihai Park in Beijing where we, a band of fifth graders, sat around in a quiet corner talking about what we would like to be when we grew up: scientists, engineers, and artists were common aspirations.

In a few years the Cultural Revolution would engulf the country. Many of us would act savagely, destroying poetry books, gramophone records, and scientific equipment—things we had cherished in our childhood. The constructive ideals so beautifully articulated by my classmates seemed to have disappeared without a trace. What happened? How could we explain this incredible transformation?

The Years of Critical Importance

By carefully retracing each critical step in our educational experience, we discern a significant turn about 1964. Ideological indoctrination of students intensified while, at the same time, forceful efforts were made to eliminate any unrevolutionary thoughts and sentiments students might harbor. Called "the revolutionizing movement" in both our secondary schools, this same initiative took place on many school campuses in Beijing and across the country. It amounted to a thought reform that targeted teenagers like us. One critical outcome was the successful undoing of the humanist strand that had existed in our earlier education. The complicated reasons for this remarkable turn in our education must be considered within the context of broader domestic and international politics around this time. Suffice it to say that, with hindsight, the revolutionizing movement and similar campaigns served as a prelude to the Cultural Revolution. They effectively groomed our generation for the ensuing political upheaval.

The impact of such political events has been largely overlooked by other writers.[6] To highlight them illuminates the *contingency* of change. It provides a contextualized and more historically specific explanation for the students' puzzling behavior. For me, it has clarified long-standing questions about my generation.

Both Ma Xiaodong and I note a change in our appearance during the revolutionizing movement. We began to wear loose fitting pants, dark-colored jackets and short straight hair. Eliminating gender distinctions was never articulated as a goal of the movement, but to be a revolutionary implicitly meant to look like a man. At a stage when adolescent girls usually become interested in their physical appearance, we turned away from femininity. Now with sharpened gender awareness, we recognize that the change in gender standards at this time was consequential. It forecast the arrival of female Red Guards who wore army uniforms with broad leather belts, which could conveniently serve as weapons to beat up class enemies.

Both of us went to key[7] secondary schools in Beijing. At the outbreak of the Cultural Revolution we found ourselves in the eye of the storm. From such schools the earliest Red Guards emerged and the first wave of violence occurred. This has provided us with a special vantage point to consider the experiences of our generation. Both of us had difficulty returning to this tumultuous time. It was especially hard for Ma Xiaodong as she had to confront disturbing incidents long buried in memory.[8] It was courageous of her to do so.

Ordinary versus Extraordinary

Traumatic as the Cultural Revolution was for us, our history did not begin or end with it. Nor did our life experiences always revolve around politics. Most of the recent Chinese memoirs tend to focus on the political life during the Mao years. Their recollections of the PRC history generally consist of a series of devastating political campaigns climaxed by the Cultural Revolution. What is missing from this narrow lens is the texture of everyday life and the multiple shades of gray in a huge society. It is certainly hard to draw a clear demarcation between the public and the private in China of the 1950s and 1960s, but to say that everyday life disappeared also misses the point,[9] since it ignores millions of people's actual life experiences in different situations.

Many of our most cherished memories derive from everyday life happenings. Ma Xiaodong recalls the routine Sunday trips her family made to a nearby park where her parents sipped tea while she and her brother ran about playing. I remember the many Saturday evenings I spent with friends in the auditorium of the compound where my family resided. Most of the films and art performances I saw in my childhood were shown there. Even to this day my heart warms whenever I hear the light melody that always accompanied the audience's departure at evening's end.

Urban Chinese society was profoundly transformed after the founding of the PRC. While the state significantly altered the daily life of ordinary citizens, the people themselves also contributed to its making. Ordinary, mundane details of everyday life are no less important and revealing than extraordinary events. Without the former life would be far from complete.

Even the Cultural Revolution was unable to suffocate music, literature, friendship, love, and thought from daily life. After the initial turmoil in the summer of 1966, an undercurrent of youth culture or rather counterculture emerged among some Beijing teenagers that reaffirmed mundane pursuits in everyday life and implicitly defied the political ethos of the day. It survived and even blossomed as many of our generation subsequently left cities for the countryside to receive reeducation from the peasants. An appreciation of this remarkable yet little noticed phenomenon is important for an understanding of the paradox of the Cultural Revolution and the richness of human story.[10]

As an urban generation we came of age in rural China. During this time many of us made reconnections with the humanist values of our childhood. The dawning of the reform era (1978–present) at the end of the Cultural Revolution saw us intellectually and emotionally ready to embrace the New Age. We were never the same easily inflammable teenagers. The ten years witnessed the remarkable growing-up of many of us into sober and thinking adults. Members of our generation once again played vanguard roles in the New Age, pushing for economic reform, political liberalization, and cultural openness. Twice did this generation make a mark in history; the first time as tools of "the great leader," but the second time as agents of historical change. The inclusion of the dynamic 1980s in our account—a decade that witnessed profound political, economic, and cultural transformation, demonstrates the unique journey made by a generation capable of regenerating itself and in turn regenerating their country. In this respect Ma Xiaodong's story is more telling than mine, as she was an active participant in the then unfolding "thought emancipation" campaign that left a great liberating impact on the society.

An Open-ended Quest

To make sense of the past, our starting point is the present. Years of living in the United States have given us a critical distance, an "insider out" perspective, and a broader worldview with which to reflect upon our past. Rather than a linear "tragedy–triumph–freedom" structure of narrative common to many Chinese memoirs,[11] ours is an open-ended quest, as we know that nowhere in the world has human history reached an "end."[12]

One way to get a perspective on our own lives was to relate them to the lives of our parents and grandparents. This task, however, was not as simple and straightforward as it might appear. We never knew our grandparents and until recently had little interest in knowing about them. As members of "exploiting classes," they were swept into "the historical dust pin" after the founding of the PRC. As for our parents, we never questioned their decisions to join the communist revolution in their youth until in recent years when the revolution itself was being questioned both in China and in the world. Our predicament is typical of many Chinese who find themselves confused about twentieth-century Chinese history in this global capitalist age.

As a student of history, I am troubled by the repeated rounds of sweeping historical negation in twentieth-century China,[13] which once bleached memories of our grandparents and is now bleaching memories of our parents and even us. Many young Chinese see their country's history beginning with the launching of the economic reform in the late 1970s; everything prior is prehistory and makes little sense. Sadly, a country known for its thousands of years of continuous history now is suffering from a broken sense of history.

Under the circumstances, to include the stories of our parents and grandparents at the beginning of our account is not just a conventional tribute to past generations. Rather, it demonstrates our effort to rescue historical memories. It also reflects our conscious decision to set our stories in the larger context of the ongoing modern transformation in China, in which, as we now recognize, each generation has played a part.

Quite a number of years have passed since we taped our conversations. The current narrative is a fusion of oral historical material and memoirist writing. The relaxed, interactive conversational format helped us establish rapport that was indispensable for our kind of project. We were virtually strangers when we began this project. We became good friends by the end. It was in a trusting and mutually respectful atmosphere that the subjects of adolescent sexual fantasies, personal involvement in violence in the Cultural Revolution, and encounter of homosexual friendship surfaced, matters that had been buried deeply in memory and had never been shared with anyone else. Meanwhile, our conversations naturally led us to compare and contrast with each other's experiences and that in turn made us gain greater self-awareness and deepened our self-reflection. The experience was intellectually illuminating, emotionally assuring, and mutually beneficial.

If the oral history approach helped us ask questions that had not been asked and collect reminiscences that otherwise would have been lost,[14] it also triggered our curiosity to probe deeper into certain past events. Ma Xiaodong persuaded her father to let her read an account he wrote years ago about his wife's suffering in the heat of the Cultural Revolution, while I found out more about the details of my school leader's brutal death. This was a tremendous learning process. From conversation to investigation our understanding of the past was markedly broadened and deepened. The memoirist writing we subsequently did contained results of our various inquires. It also gave us the opportunity to add other additional materials and to contemplate issues at greater leisure and in more depth.

Writing, as it turned out, was not merely desirable but also necessary for the survival of this book, since a third person, who had participated in the original recording, eventually withdrew. Rather than giving up the project, Ma Xiaodong and I decided to proceed. We needed to fill the void left by the third voice and recast the original narrative now that the personal dynamics changed. The subsequent integration of the two genres of oral history and memoirist writing rescued *and* enriched our project.

Both the original oral transcript and much of the memoirist writing were in Chinese. Translation into English has involved framing the materials for a Western audience that presumably doesn't know much about modern Chinese history. Things that likely invoke ready responses from informed Chinese readers may hardly mean anything to people in the West. I had to sacrifice some details that were revealing in the Chinese context but would require lengthy and complicated explanations for the Western audience. Most of the time, however, I was able to "translate," which entailed not just a change of language but often a built-in process of interpreting a complex history. Yet it was not just about overcoming obstacles. Occasionally I was able to "ride" on English vocabulary that was more effective in denoting certain events than what was available in Chinese. A telling example was the usage of "youth culture" and "counterculture" to depict the political activities and personal lifestyles of a small but highly visible group of disillusioned Beijing former Red Guards. Although there were obvious differences between the Chinese youngsters and the American "hippies" of 1960s, in both cases the youths were rebelling against established political and cultural norms in their respective countries.

Following the first chapter on our family histories, our own life stories are divided into five parts by chronological order. At the beginning of each chapter / section there is a short introduction to familiarize the reader with historical background. Some chapters involve more interaction between Ma and me; in other chapters we tell our stories separately. I have retained the conversational style to be true to the original flavor of the recording. Hopefully this format captures the often diverse perspectives of two Chinese women who in many ways were cut from the same cloth.

"Even If You Cut It, It Will Not Come Apart"

Ma Xiaodong and I have felt a growing need to reconcile ourselves with the realities of our grandparents' existence. Now that we have come a long way from our naïve youth, we want to dig deeper into our roots, piecing together family histories that were broken by political exigencies. Learning about our grandparents has helped us understand our parents more fully. Growing up at a time when revolution was taken for granted, we never felt it necessary to ask our parents, "Why did you join the revolution?" We raise this question now, at a moment when the appeal of revolution is receding worldwide and some leading Chinese intellectuals have bid it farewell.[1] We ask the question with the realization that revolution not only shaped the lives of our parents but also left an indelible imprint on us. "Even if you cut it, it will not come apart"—this line from a tenth-century Chinese poem captures the reality of our inseverable connections both to our grandparents whose class identifications made them targets of the revolution, and our parents who forged much of their lives with the revolution.

Ye Weili's Family

YE: In the fall of 1998 I made a trip to Yan'an, the headquarters of the Chinese Communist Party (CCP) in the 1930s and 1940s.

MA: Was it a revolutionary pilgrimage? Yan'an is a sacred place for the Chinese revolution. I've been there myself.

YE: I felt more like an archaeologist trying to uncover a layer of the bygone past. My parents lived there briefly in the late 1930s and then for a large part of the 1940s. I wanted to trace the footsteps of my parents, especially those of my mother, who passed away in 1996.

One place I went to was Qingliang Mountain. Xinhua News Agency[2]—my parents' work unit until their retirement—was located there during the Sino-Japanese War. There was a small exhibition hall to commemorate the revolutionary past of the news organization. Going over the exhibit, I was drawn to a photo in which I recognized some colleagues of my parents. Among them I found the fathers of some childhood playmates. Wearing army uniforms, they looked no more than 30 year-old. Looking at these strangely young yet familiar faces, I was amazed by the physical resemblance of my friends to their fathers. Suddenly a thought dawned on me: the people in this old photo were all my parental figures. My generation was connected to them by blood and flesh. Through them we had an inseparable tie to that event known as the Chinese revolution.

Exiting the exhibition hall, I came out into bright sunshine. Across from the Qingliang Mountain was the famous Pagoda Mountain, the symbol of Yan'an during wartime. Staring at this revolutionary icon and hearing the busy city noise below me, I asked myself, "After more than sixty years, what does the revolution leave us?"

An old man interrupted my contemplation. Possibly thinking that this solemn-looking middle-aged woman was suffering from personal troubles, he asked if I'd like to have my fortune told. These days most people climbed up to Qingliang Mountain not to pay tribute to the revolutionary relics but to visit a Buddhist temple. It would never have occurred to the old fortuneteller that I was musing about the legacy of the revolution.

MA: Like you, I've also wondered about how the revolution has turned out. In recent years, I have often bitterly criticized the CCP in front of my father. I resented the party's role in the great famine of the early 1960s and the subsequent Cultural Revolution; I also blamed the party for the widespread corruption now eroding the Chinese society. I knew my harsh criticism hurt my father's feelings. In his youth, he fought hard alongside his comrades for a better society. I certainly understood his insistence that their efforts were worthwhile. As a matter of fact, I often feel the urge to find justification for the revolution. I want to defend my father and his comrades in history.

YE: I don't want to defend anyone, but I'd like to understand why the revolution occurred and what it meant for the people who took part in it, because it was such as a consequential event in twentieth-century Chinese history. It is up to us to sort out its mixed legacy. I am curious what led my parents to join the revolution in the first place. My paternal grandfather was a capitalist and my maternal grandfather was a landlord, precisely the targets of a communist revolution.

My father once told me of two encounters he had as a child, both of which have helped answer my question. My father's family lived in the treaty-port city of Tianjin. A familiar scene in his childhood was people begging in the streets. One day he and his brother were playing outside the gate of their home. A father and daughter in ragged clothes were walking in their direction. Seeing the well-dressed boys in front of a wealthy residence, the father pleaded for food. This was nothing unusual. What took my father aback was what the little girl said to her father, "Don't kowtow. They won't give," in a clearly defiant voice. It left such a deep impression on my father that he still remembered it word for word more than 60 years later. On another occasion my father was shocked to find a beggar hurting his own body to induce sympathy from passersby. He beat his chest with a piece of broken brick and blood was all over his body. Incidents like these made my father see injustice in society, even though he himself lived a cushioned life.

In fact, injustice also existed in his own family. My grandfather was an old-style bureaucrat-turned-banker and industrialist in the treaty-port Tianjin region. You may say he was a member of the emerging bourgeoisie in China. But he continued to be conservative in his private life. He had a wife and two concubines. All the children were born to his concubines. The first concubine was once a maid in an official's family and was given by the family as a "gift" to my grandfather. The second concubine had been a local opera singer; she was my grandmother.

My grandmother must have come from a very humble background. My father and his siblings had no contact with their mother's natal family. When their uncle came for a visit, he only stayed in the gatekeeper's room. Among his three wives, my grandfather favored my grandmother the most. After coming back from work, he often lay on a rattan chair and my grandmother would read him "mandarin-duck and butterfly" novels.[3] It amuses me to picture my grandmother reading romantic stories to my grandfather.

My grandfather didn't get along with his first wife and didn't even speak to her much. But as *taitai* (lady of the house), she managed the family finances. The children had to address her as mother and their own mother as aunt. The position of the two concubines in the family was not much higher than that of servants. *Taitai* cursed them whenever she felt like it. Even though there were many servants in the household, the two concubines had to wait on *taitai*. They only stopped doing so when their sons were older. Moreover, they never ate at the same table with their husband and not even with their grown-up sons. Instead, they ate with their younger children and the food was not as good. Years later an uncle observed to me that the fact several boys from this well-to-do family ended up either joining the CCP or becoming sympathizers of the revolutionary party had a lot to do with their mothers' pathetic status in the family.[4]

On her deathbed, my grandmother expressed the wish to wear a red dress when she died. By custom, only a properly married woman could wear the red color at death. When *taitai* gave her the permission, my grandmother struggled to sit up and kowtowed, saying, "Thank you, *taitai*."[5] She died the next day. But even in death, my grandmother remained a concubine. She was not buried with my grandfather. Her modest grave was located behind the elaborate graves of *laoye* (the master) and *taitai*.

If what my father observed at home and in society made him aware of injustice, it was at school that he received his initial political education. My father went to Nankai in Tianjin, a Westernized secondary school run by a liberal-minded Chinese educator.[6] He entered Nankai at the time the Japanese had occupied Manchuria and were encroaching into the northern China plain. Near the school campus was a Japanese military camp and the students could hear cannon fire from their classrooms. A famous contemporary saying echoed my father's experience at the time, "There is not a quiet corner to place a student's desk throughout northern China." Feeling frustrated by Jiang Jieshi's unwillingness to confront the Japanese invaders, an increasing number of educated young men and women placed their hope in the communists. Under the influence of such people my father became a member of a left-leaning youth organization with ties to the CCP and took part in the communists-led December 9th Student Movement in 1935.[7] When the Sino-Japanese War finally broke out in 1937, he chose to follow the communists. Many other educated youth also joined the Communist Party after the war began.

My mother was among them. She came from a big landlord family in Hebei province. It was my grandmother's decision that all the girls in the family should go to school. In the 1920s and 1930s, it was still rather unusual for girls to be educated, especially if you consider the experiences of my paternal aunts. Even though my grandfather provided the best modern education for his sons, he only allowed his daughters to study at home with private tutors. They were taught traditional female virtues of docility and subservience. Tianjin was a Westernized city and my grandfather was a member of the bourgeoisie, yet he was so conservative about his daughters' education. By comparison, my maternal grandmother was quite *kaiming* (enlightened), a phrase my mother often used to praise her mother. My mother always talked about her family and her childhood with warm feelings, which, if you think about it, was politically incorrect because her family belonged to the "exploiting class."

As a high school student in Beiping (now Beijing), my mother also participated in the December 9th movement and threw herself enthusiastically in the patriotic student activities at school. When the war broke out, she said to her niece, who was about the same age, "You go to a safe place and get married. I will go fight the Japanese." Years later in the United States, I met this woman whom I call "big cousin." She looked at least ten years younger than my mother, though she was actually slightly older. She showed me photos of her family during their recent trip to Europe. I cannot help comparing the different life courses my mother and her niece followed—big cousin becoming a housewife and living a rather cushioned life, my mother taking the nobler path at the moment of national crisis and paying a high personal price for it.

I have seen a photo of my mother at the beginning of the war. Clad in an air force cap and an army uniform, she looked handsome and valiant. She had turned herself into a "woman warrior," good at both horsemanship and marksmanship. Around this time she changed her given name from the feminine "shizhen" to the gender neutral and grand-sounding "tian" (天 / sky), partly to protect her family left behind in the enemy-occupied territory, but also to signal the beginning of a new life that seemed to offer boundless possibility.

The war altered my mother's life tremendously. She became crippled and her health was irreparably damaged. The direct cause was not war but childbirth. I used to tell people that my mother was wounded in a battlefield, because I felt childbirth sounded trivial. Only in recent years have I begun to appreciate my mother's experience in the war as a woman.

My mother gave birth to a baby girl in the winter of 1941, which happened to be the most trying year for the Chinese resistance during the war. The Japanese had just launched a major mopping-up campaign in the Xingxian region in Shanxi province where my parents were working. Since it was well-known that wherever the Japanese soldiers went they would leave a trail of blood and gore, my mother hurriedly crossed the Yellow River to get to a safer place. She walked 60 *li* (about 20 miles), unaided and nine-month pregnant, in the grip of a bitter winter.

MA: Why didn't your father accompany her?

YE: He had to stay behind to participate in a counter-mopping-up campaign. When the Japanese finally left (after killing over 1,300 people and destroying almost 6,000 houses in the Xingxian county), my father went to look for my mother. He had an ominous premonition that something terrible had happened. He found my mother lying on an unheated *kang* (brick platform-bed) in an icy-cold cave room. She had caught childbirth fever and was in a coma. My sister was left to the care of a village woman, who fed her milk made from black soybean. Coincidentally, *heidou* (黑豆 / black soybean) was the name my parents had chosen for my sister. Because of a shortage of food supply, my mother had eaten a lot of black soybeans during her pregnancy. When my father saw my sister, she was as thin as a small cat. A few days later she died. My mother was unaware of my sister's death as she herself was at death's door. Eventually she was able to pull through, but the incident left her permanently disabled.

Besides the childbirth fever, my mother also developed serious arthritis. After her recovery from the fever, she was taken to a nearby field hospital to treat her arthritis. This so-called hospital was operated in a rundown peasant house with few qualified medical personnel. After putting a device called a Thomas cast around my mother's badly swollen right leg, the people there left her lay in bed for months. By the time they remembered to remove the cast, my mother's leg had become as rigid as a stick.

When I first heard this story in the 1960s, I took it as a revolutionary legend about hardships in war. These days I've begun to see a gendered dimension: pregnancy, childbirth, and even menstruation could put women in life-threatening predicaments during war.

My mother left that terrible field hospital on a stretcher. She was carried to Yan'an where there was a better-equipped hospital. After she finally arrived in Yan'an many days later, the doctors in the hospital told her that they could do nothing to help her—it was too late.

To make matters worse, my father was detained as a suspected Nationalist spy during the Rescue Campaign.[8] A friend who had known my mother before she fell ill visited her around this time. My mother was poised. She shed no tears and uttered no complaints. Since this friend had come from a region where the material condition was even worse than Yan'an, my mother dragged her bad leg around to cook an egg and tomato dish for her. Another friend often found my mother sunbathing her leg when the weather was nice. She still looked beautiful even though she was crippled. This was the most taxing time in my mother's life, yet she maintained her grace and dignity. The image of my mother sitting in front of a cave in Yan'an has been engraved in my mind and has sustained me during some tough moments in my own life.

My father said he only saw my mother cry once after she became crippled. It was on the day of the Japanese surrender (August 15, 1945). That day the entire city of Yan'an turned into a sea of joy. Vendors threw candies and dried fruits into the air, shouting, "We won! We won!" Yet my mother cried, and she cried hard. The war was finally over, but she was no longer her old self.

MA: Your mother's story touches me, but it also makes me wonder about the priorities of the CCP in war time. Their belief that "the interest of the revolution is above everything else" precluded humanitarian concerns. I wonder what would have happened if your father had been wounded or fallen ill. Perhaps your mother would have been asked to accompany him to a safe place.

YE: I've been thinking about these questions myself. In recent years my father brought up the subject of my mother's illness a number of times. It seemed that the older he got, the harder it was for him to make peace with my mother's tragic fate. When he talked about it, he always remarked that "your mother's health was ruined just like that," as if he still could not believe it. But he always added that the war situation made it out of the question for him to leave the front with my mother.

For many years, I wanted to trace the route my mother took on her way to give birth to my sister. The wish became especially strong after her death in 1996. When I finally made the trip in 1998, I started in Xingxian, Shanxi province, and ended in Yan'an, Shaanxi province. In 1941 my mother walked from the Xingxian county site to Heiyukuo, a village by the riverside, to cross the Yellow River. I got a ride in a jeep to cover the same distance. Most of the road was still unpaved. On one side was the winding riverbed of the Weifen River, on the other tall, rocky mountains. The road was so narrow at times that I was afraid our jeep would fall into the steep riverbed. The Yellow River at Heiyukuo was more than 300 meters wide. Even on a windless autumn day the water looked rough. No wonder it had served as a natural barrier during the war. When my mother crossed the river, it was winter time. My mother's passage must have been made especially treacherous by the ice heaves that had transformed the frozen Yellow River. How fortunate she managed to get across.

On the other side of the river was Shaanxi province, where in a village still miles away my sister was born and soon died. Not knowing which village it was, I continued my journey southward to Yan'an. It was a memorable experience. At first I was quite annoyed. The driver of our van chose to travel on a dirt road instead of paved highway. The motor vehicle stirred up so much dust that I could hardly breathe. It stopped constantly to pick up passengers. At one point somebody even brought piglets aboard. I could have taken a much more comfortable tour bus going a different route, but the driver convinced me his van would be faster. I felt cheated.

What eventually calmed me down was the grand scenery of the northern Shanbei plateau. Our driver took the path less traveled. We climbed up and down narrow mountain roads and our van was about the only moving object in sight. When we reached the top of a mountain, an endless sea of high plateaus lined the horizon. The view was more magnificent than the Grand Canyon.

But nature posed a formidable challenge for the people living there. There was so little arable land that the peasants had to utilize every inch of it, making terraced fields wherever humanly possible, even on mountaintops. As a sent-down youth during the Cultural Revolution I was no stranger to the destitution in rural northern China, but the impoverished conditions on the yellow earth still dazzled me. I was amazed by the rugged survival skills of the local people. I also realized how incredibly tough it must have been for the many urban youth who came to this part of China during the war time. In the case of my mother, she passed through this baffling region twice—once on foot and the second time on a stretcher.

One place I wanted to visit in Yan'an was the site of an old brewery. Since no doctors could help her, my mother decided to help herself. She learned that the distilled residue might reduce the symptoms of arthritis, so she moved near the brewery and everyday covered her leg with hot hops. This folk remedy worked. People had predicted that my mother would have to rely on crutches for the rest of her life, but she eventually managed to stand up on her two feet unaided.

Through her own experience, my mother knew very well that life was filled with adversity, but she never gave up striving. This spirit stayed with her until the last days of her life, when her whole body was swollen and she was constantly in a coma. One day I heard her sleep talking, "Don't be afraid; don't be afraid," in an amazingly sturdy voice for a dying person. In her long trying life she must have said the same words to herself so many times that they had entered her subconsciousness.

My mother was known for her kindness. Although she was from a landlord family, she was very respectful of laboring people. This trait also shone in her final days. Since she had broken her hip and couldn't move, we hired a helper in the hospital. When my mother was awake she always thanked the person, a peasant woman from Anhui province. She thanked her in the old-fashioned way: holding her two hands in front of her chest and moving them up and down. Sometimes the life support tubes prevented her from moving her upper body. Then she would wave her feet in a gentle manner, and we all understood she was saying "thanks." She had lost much of her mind because of Alzheimer's disease, yet she still knew how to be grateful.

My mother was cremated at Babaoshan. When we went to get her ashes, a person asked, "Was she a party member?" I said, "Yes," and he handed over a Communist Party flag the size of a handkerchief. I put it in my pocket without giving it much thought. Afterwards we went to a cemetery to temperately store my mother's ashes there. After placing the simple ash container in a storage room, we were about to leave. Then I paused. It was below zero outside and the room was not heated. Mother must be cold. I remembered the party flag and took it out from my pocket. My mother's life had been interwoven with this organization ever since her youth. Gently, I covered the container with the flag. No matter what I thought of the party, this was not a moment for judgment.

Ma Xiaodong's Family

MA: My mother grew up without parents: her mother died when she was a baby and she never knew her father. When I was small, my maternal grandfather was a mysterious figure to me. My mother never mentioned a word about him, which made me curious. Later I managed to find out some facts. My grandfather came from a poor family in rural Henan. Because he was extremely bright, the local government supported his education. After graduating from college he won a scholarship to study in the United States. When he returned to China, he taught in a college in Beijing. He moved to the southwestern city Kunming after the outbreak of the Sino-Japanese War, and taught college there for the rest of his life.

He got married before going to college. It was an arranged marriage. When he went abroad, my grandmother stayed behind and waited for him for many years. After he came back, my grandparents had my mother. Right after my mother's birth, however, my grandmother discovered that her husband had taken a mistress, an educated urban woman. This news so devastated her that my grandmother committed suicide. My mother was barely one month old. Her uncle took her into his home even though he was a poor farmer and could hardly feed his own family. After negotiation, my grandfather agreed to pay some child support.

In the summer of 1966, my parents received an unexpected letter from my grandfather. My mother didn't respond because she could not forgive her father for abandoning her as a baby. Besides, the timing of the old man's long-overdue reconciliation could not have been worse, as the Cultural Revolution was raging throughout the country.

When the letter arrived, I glanced at the envelope and saw the name of the college where my grandfather worked. In the fall of 1968 I left Beijing to go to Yunnan province as a sent-down youth. The capitol city Kunming was the last stop of our long train ride, where we stayed for a few days before continuing our journey. I decided to use this interval to look for my grandfather. At the college gate I asked the security guard if my grandfather still worked there. He answered in a stern voice, "Yes, but he is a reactionary academic authority figure." I should have known better that college professors across the country almost all had been labeled as such by this time. I made another attempt to contact him and his family in the early 1990s, but again to no avail.

I wanted to find him because he was my mother's father. In his letter to my mother, I later learned, he had asked about us. I would like to tell him that I also came to the United States to study. I think he would be pleased to hear this. Perhaps my mother never forgave her father, but I understand why he couldn't get along with my grandmother. The gap between a man educated in America and an illiterate countrywoman was simply too great. But there were things I could not forgive him about. Why didn't he take my mother to Beijing to live with his new family? Even if he had to leave my mother in the countryside, he could have gone back to see his daughter. But he didn't even make one visit.

As I think about it, similar fate also happened to my paternal aunts. Both my father and his two brothers had arranged marriages before they joined the revolution. Later they all remarried. In the case of my father, his first wife died before he met my mother. But my two uncles' wives were alive when their husbands left them to marry their female comrades. The women and their children simply continued to live in the old family home.

Many years after his remarriage, one uncle went back to his home village for a visit. His first wife thought that even after divorce she was still his woman, so she made up a bed for him in her bedroom. But my uncle moved his bedding to another room, leaving my aunt crying quietly by herself. Luckily, my paternal grandfather was very kind. He continued to treat the two divorced women as his daughters-in-law and took good care of the grandchildren.

My grandfather was a farmer, but he was also a learned scholar in the Confucian school. The family lived in a village not far from Qufu, the home-town of Confucius. My grandfather admired historical figures who demonstrated *qijie* (气节 / an unbending spirit in the face of adversity). His favorite hero was Wen Tianxiang, a Song dynasty official who refused to submit to Mongol invaders. This father's value influenced the sons' decision to join the resistance forces against the Japanese.

My grandfather used to be the village head. After the Japanese occupied the region, he refused to collaborate with the enemy and resigned from the post. For a long time during the war, whenever there was a market day in the nearby town, he would take his family there and set up a stand to serve people free hot tea. Some members of the family were not happy about it. They had to get up early, spend money on firewood and tea leaves, yet did not earn a single penny. But my grandfather insisted. He was hoping that his good deeds would protect his three sons at the front. After the war was over, the local government presented my grandfather with a *bian* (匾 / a horizontal inscribed board) to praise his patriotic spirit.

During the Land Reform,[9] my grandfather was classified as rich peasant, a member of the "exploiting class." Yet the family was only rich in a relative sense, since the region as a whole was very poor. During the Cultural Revolution, my father's work unit sent people to his home village to investigate his family. When they came back, they quietly told my father that they had seen the *bian* my grandfather received for his exemplary behavior during the war.

In the 1950s, my grandfather visited us in Beijing a few times. He was a quiet old peasant man and I found nothing to say to him. I was too young then to realize that everybody's life has a story.

Influenced by his father, my father was a diligent student. Eventually he surpassed my grandfather as the leading scholar in the village. Recognizing his son's talent, my grandfather recommended my father to be the village schoolteacher. After teaching my father liked to spend his spare time in a quiet spot on Mt. Tai. He often brought books with him to read aloud. When he did it, it sounded like singing punctuated by rhythm. As a child I heard him "singing" the documents he had brought home to read. I was always amused.

My father had a bizarre experience as a child. In accordance with the local custom, my grandparents had arranged a marriage for him when he was a small boy. When my father was about eight years old, the girl died. One day my father was accompanied by a relative to the cemetery where the girl was buried to "marry" her, since she was considered a member of my father's family even in death. By going to the cemetery to marry her, my father brought her back home. Otherwise she would be a homeless ghost roaming about the local community.

My father had a second arranged marriage when he was in his late teens. This wife was a few years older. After giving birth to a baby, my big elder brother, she contracted a breast infection and soon died. In those days even a minor illness could cause death.

When the war broke out, my father joined the communists to fight against the Japanese. He had been dissatisfied with the Nationalist government's policy toward the Japanese and had been under the influence of left-wing literature such as the works of Lu Xun.[10]

My parents met during the war. My father was young, good-looking, and known among his colleagues for his literary talent. More than one woman was interested in him, but he had his standards. One day he heard that a new woman comrade was assigned to work at the local resistance organization and somehow he remembered her name. Then on a beautiful spring day they met on the road. In a memorial piece he wrote after my mother's death, my father described his first impression of her: "She was walking hastily; her face was nicely shaped and red with sweat, and there was a kind expression on it. She looked healthy and sturdy and was simply dressed." Two years later they got married.

In 1946 my mother gave birth to a son, my little elder brother. Soon the war broke out between the communists and the Nationalists. My parents had to send my brother to my paternal grandfather. My brother rejoined my parents when I was a little girl. I was very close to this brother, but there were moments when I wished I had a little elder sister. Only much later did I learn that I indeed had a sister who was born after my brother. Because of the war situation my parents had to leave her with a peasant family. After 1949 they went back to look for her, only to find that she had died of illness.

* * *

Compared with our sisters, we were lucky to be born at a time of peace, after the founding of the PRC. My earliest photo was taken soon after my birth. My mother was sitting on a hospital bed holding me. She looked weak, but she was smiling. My sister had not been so fortunate to have a nice hospital welcoming her to the world.

"Flowers of the Nation"

In the 1950s, there was a popular children's movie called "Flowers of the Nation." A well-known scene in the movie was a group of youngsters enjoying themselves at the end of a school day in Beijing's scenic Beihai Park. Caressed by a light breeze, the children are rowing boats on a beautiful lake surrounded by green trees and red palace walls. This is certainly an idealized image of urban childhood in the 1950s, yet the notion of being flowers of the nation was taken to heart by many people in our generation.

Both Ma and I started to attend boarding kindergarten at a tender age, staying there during the week and only rejoining our parents on weekend. When we were in elementary school, our life revolved around "ban jiti" (班集体 / class collective) for the entire six years. Meanwhile, the residential compounds where each of our families lived embodied a communal ideal. Even if "collective" and "communal" characterized our upbringing, we both agree that family life was vitally important for us, although our families differed from each other markedly.

* * *

The Boarding Kids

YE: I went to a kindergarten that was run by my parents' work unit, Xinhua. It was not unusual for large work units to provide childcare for their employees. In my memory, kindergarten was a fun place. My class had about twenty "*xiao pengyou*" (小朋友 / little friends). We all slept in a large room, each child on a small bed. During naptime, there were always some naughty boys who would do everything to disturb other kids' sleep. We had three teachers. I wouldn't say they were like mothers, but they were generally caring and responsible. My brother, who was one year younger than me, also went to the same kindergarten, but he didn't like it as much. He always made a big fuss when it was time to go back on Sunday afternoons. Once he even hid under a bed and refused to come out. After I started elementary school my parents switched him to a day-care center near home.

My kindergarten was located in the suburbs of Beijing. Our simple one-story brick houses were surrounded by woods and it felt like wilderness. Thumb-sized frogs hopped all over the dirt ground while snakes hid in the grass. One day we caught a hedgehog that had wandered into our dining room. We tried to stick dates on to its back but it quickly ran away. Our environment fit nicely with the fairy-tale world depicted in the children's books we were reading—a world inhabited by Snow White, Little Red Riding Hood, and Frog Prince. In this fantacy world, animals lived in wooden cabins, spoke human language, and got along well with people. I carried this fairy-tale imagery with me for many years to come.

There was a huge flowerbed in front of our kindergarten. We girls discovered that balsam flowers could be used for nail polish. We smashed the red flowers and pressed the paste on our nails. Then we wrapped our nails in leaves for awhile until the nails turned red.

MA: As a little girl I also liked to look pretty. I had a flowered dress I liked so much that, at night, I would fold it carefully and put it under my pillow. This was my way of ironing.

YE: My kindergarten teachers paid a lot of attention to their appearance. One young teacher had a pair of red leather shoes that she liked to wear on Saturdays to go to dance parties. I knew this because I overheard the teachers chatting. Even after so many years, whenever I see a young woman in red leather shoes, I think of that teacher. I still vaguely remember what she looked like, but I'm afraid I have no memory of my mother's face at the time.

MA: My early memory of my mother is also vague. As I think about it, it might have something to do with the fact that she always wore plain simple clothes. Nothing distinguished her.

Your kindergarten sounds like a lovely place. I don't have a clear memory of my kindergarten, and what I do remember is not so cheerful. Like yours, my kindergarten also was run by my father's work unit, the Ministry of Commerce. It was located in a courtyard in downtown Beijing and it only had a small playground with one pair of swings. When I was there, I guess

I was happy. The teachers taught us to sing and dance and I was always chosen as the lead dancer. But I also missed my parents terribly. My happiest moment was when they came to take me home on Saturday. Like your brother, I dreaded going back to the kindergarten on Sunday afternoon. One day as I was walking with my father, he jokingly remarked, "Look, your kindergarten is just around the corner." I grabbed my father's hand and begged, "Don't take me there. Today is not the day!" Because my mother was off attending a cadres' training school far away from home, it usually was my father who picked me up on Saturdays. One weekend neither of my parents could come, so they arranged to have a kindergarten teacher take me to her home. I felt sorry for myself and could hardly sleep the whole night.

YE: I liked my kindergarten because we also heard a lot of stories. I can still remember the folk tales such as "The Five Brothers of the Liu Family" and "The Magic Painter Ma Liang."

MA: I also remember those stories. The five Liu brothers all had special abilities. One had legs that could extend very long, another could withstand the hit of any weapon, and the third could speak animals' language, and so on. Together they outsmarted a nasty official. Magic Painter Ma Liang had a brush that could transform anything he drew into real objects: food, houses, animals, you name it. He used this magic power to help many needy people, but he refused to serve the greedy landlord.

YE: I also remember the animated children's movie "The Arrogant General," which was set in ancient China. After a victory in a big battle, the general became arrogant and lazy. His weapon got rusty and his soldiers stayed idle. When the enemy returned, he was caught unprepared and his troops were badly defeated. This tale taught diligence and modesty without a particular ideological bend.

The first book I read on my own was "The Turnip Has Come Back." In the story everybody put somebody else first, beginning with Little Rabbit. It was in wintertime and there was a shortage of food. Thinking that the animal living next door must be hungry, Little Rabbit placed his last turnip outside his neighbor's cabin. Then the turnip began to travel from one animal's home to another since everybody thought that someone else needed it more. In the end, it came back to Little Rabbit.

MA: My favorite stories were romantic fairy tales in which love transcended boundaries of wealth or class: a fairy maiden falling for a poor cowherd; a prince enduring many hardships to find his peasant girl friend, and so on. These tales sowed seeds of idealism and romanticism in me. Back then I read everything. It didn't matter whether it was proletarian or bourgeois.

YE: We were exposed to arts and literature from many parts of the world. Once an Indian dance troupe performed in Beijing and a scene from their play appeared on a magazine cover. I was fascinated by the gorgeous costumes and beautiful make-up of the performers. When I was about ten, a new theatre was built near our compound. My parents took us to see *The Miser* and *The Blunderer* by Moliere. Children's books such as *Grimms Fairy Tales* were very popular. My favorite author was Hans Christian Anderson and I devoured every piece I could find by him. I was deeply touched by his "The Little Mermaid." The Chinese translation had a beautiful title "The Daughter of Sea" (海的女儿 / *haide nüer*). In the end of the story, Little Mermaid was faced with an agonizing situation: she would turn into bubbles the next morning unless she killed the prince and his new bride. At night, all her mermaid sisters surfaced from the sea to urge her to act. But she decided she couldn't harm the innocent couple. The next day when the sun rose, her body changed into bubbles, disappearing in the vast sea. I was moved by the humanism in the story, embodied by a beautiful mermaid.[1]

If you think about it, stories like "The Five Brothers of the Liu family" and "The Magic Painter Ma Liang" did have to be politically correct. The bad guy was either a mean landlord or an abusive official. But you could take other messages from the stories too, such as having sympathy for the poor and the dispossessed. In the 1950s our education was not yet permeated by revolutionary rhetoric as would be the case in the 1960s. This was a time when Snow White could coexist with the young revolutionary heroine Liu Hulan.[2]

MA: And the revolutionary themes were presented to us in an accessible way. I am thinking of the 1950s film "The Red Kids" (红孩子 / *hong haizi*). It was about a group of communist kids in the early 1930s during the struggle between the communists and Nationalists. Its theme song began with: "Are you ready? Let's get ready. We are members of the Communist Children's League." It's very upbeat.

Were children's ditties big in your life? Some of them conveyed political messages. They were popular during the Korean War. One ridiculed the South Korean leader Syngman Rhee and was pretty coarse. Another mocked Harry Truman. It went something like "Truman is a blowhard. He blows, he blows, and he blows a big fat balloon."

YE: But honestly, this kind of ditty didn't leave as deep an impression on me as traditional nursery rhymes, such as the one about a little rat getting caught while stealing oil and another a boy getting excited about visiting his maternal grandmother and having a good time there. They were simple, folksy, and fun.

* * *

Parenting for the Nation

Our parents were our first and foremost teachers in life. Our mothers belonged to a cohort of communist women who clad themselves in army uniforms in their youth and unisex clothes for much of the remainder of their lives. This gray image, however, fails to convey the richness of their humanity. I have long recognized my mother's monumental influence on me whereas Ma Xiaodong has become more appreciative of her mother with the passing of time. Both of us now realize that our mothers significantly molded our own womanhood. In light of our gendered consciousness, to see our mothers as women helps us cherish their memories differently. Meanwhile a gendered analysis cannot neglect the impact of the father. Ma Xiaodong's description of her father as a patriarch has made me see how liberal my father was. Both our fathers were communist cadres, yet they parented in quite different ways.

MA: My family lived close to Beihai Park so we often went there on Sundays. Our activity in the park followed the same routine. My parents sat at a spot on top of the White Pagoda Hill, drinking tea and chatting. My little elder brother and I ran all over the hill, playing hide-and-seek. After exploring every cave on the hill, we returned to our parents, soaked with sweat, asking for drinks and food. We also went to see Beijing operas, stage plays, and movies. We saw lots of foreign movies. Several were based on Shakespeare's plays, including "Hamlet." We also ate out a lot. Whenever we went out, I would get excited and cheer, "We are going out to eat! We are going out to eat!"

But there was another side to our family life. I have mixed feelings when I think of my father and his position at home. I guess it was because he often acted like a patriarch. For example, at mealtime my father always sat in the same seat. It was either my brother's or my job to put rice in his bowl even though he was sitting next to the rice pot. We had to get up and walk over to serve him. Most days my father would get a special dish, such as scrambled eggs or boiled peanuts, to go with his beer. My father rarely helped with household chores, but he was obsessed with cleanliness. This made everybody nervous. When he saw a small piece of paper on the floor, he would get upset and pick it up.

We all understood my father's position in the family and deferred to him. His mood determined the atmosphere in the home. At the dinner table if he didn't speak we all would eat quietly, nobody making a noise. If he was in good spirits, we then could talk and laugh. For a long time I thought every family was like ours until one day I visited the home of a college friend. I was astonished to see her joking with her father and the two heartily laughing together. So parents and children could relate like this!

As I think about my father now, I see two major influences that shaped his character: Confucianism and communism. While he tended to behave in an authoritarian way in daily life, he did one thing for which I will always be grateful. When I was about four years old, he asked me one day, "Which surname would you prefer, 'Song' (my father's name) or 'Ma' (my mother's name)?" I thought for a while and replied, "I want 'Ma' (also means horse) because horses can run." So I got my mother's surname. My paternal grandfather was not pleased when he learned that I had adopted my mother's family name. Not many fathers would let their daughters choose their own surname. In this respect my father was quite liberal. I think it was because he believed that ultimately we belonged to the nation, and a parent's job was to bring up the children for the good of the public. This mentality led to his more equal treatment for girls. Among his three children, my father favored me the most. I was rather spoiled. Who could share his special dishes? Me. Nobody else touched them.

I was the youngest and the only daughter. I had always been with my parents whereas my two brothers had first lived with my grandfather. Because my mother was away in school when I was small, my father spent a lot of time with me. Besides, I was an earnest student and showed a passion for whatever I did. My father liked these traits.

My mother went along with my father's patriarchal style. At the dinner table even when my father invited her to share his dishes, she would not touch them. My mother was the party secretary of a secondary school, but at home she was simply a wife and a mother. You would not know that she held a responsible position at work. When I was small, I always felt that my father's work was more important than my mother's. Although I was very close to my mother, I showed more respect for my father. With my mother I sometimes could be rude. If I thought she talked too much, I would say, "Stop, stop. You've said enough."

I think overall my parents' relationship was egalitarian. But there was no question that my father was the head of the family. My mother's role at home was just a "*xianqi liangmu*" (virtuous wife and good mother). My father would get irritated sometimes and only my mother could calm him down. Since my father had a large extended family, conflicts would arise from time to time among family members. My mother always managed to iron out the frictions and keep the family glued together. I didn't realize how important my mother was to all of us until her death and until I myself became a mother. I miss her terribly.

YE: I am still struck by the atmosphere at your family dinner table. I guess how a family spends meal time tells a lot about the family. In my home there wasn't a patriarch. My father didn't enjoy any privilege. Dinnertime was usually a joyful time for everybody. My brother and I competed with each other to report what had happened during the day while our parents listened with smiles. We were free to express our opinions and our parents never shut us down. My mother liked to give us nicknames. Among the ones she picked for me was "Ma Daha" (马大哈), a character from a famous *xiangsheng* (相声 / Chinese cross talk that resembles a stand-up comedy) known for his absent-mindedness. So you get a sense of what my mother thought of me.

Not everybody approved of the open atmosphere in my family. Once a relative invited us to see a stage play his troupe performed. Afterwards he asked my parents about their opinion. The play was set in a secondary school and was about educational reform, a hot topic at the time. Before my parents said anything, I started to offer my opinion. I was then in junior high and was familiar with the life depicted in the play. But my remarks didn't amuse this relative, who said to my parents with obvious disapproval, "Your family is too democratic."

It didn't mean that my parents would indulge our wrong doings. But even when we went astray, they still treated us with respect. When I was about eight or nine, for a while my favorite pastime after school was to hang around the general store in the Xinhua compound. What attracted me there were the candies wrapped in glittering paper, but I didn't have the money to buy them. Finally I decided to get some for myself.

MA: Stealing?

YE: Yes. I succeeded a couple of times until a neighbor saw me and told my parents. That evening after my brother went to sleep, my parents came to our bedroom and sat down by my bed. In low and gentle voices, they said, "Don't do it again. All right?"

MA: Was that all?

YE: Yes. There was no inquisition like "how many times you have done it" and so forth. None of that. And they avoided the word "stealing." After this conversation they never mentioned the incident again. I don't even know if they still remember. But I will never forget.

MA: My father would have been furious and would definitely have given me a good scolding.

YE: My father did so once. When I was in junior high I had some money on me—four or five Chinese *yuan*. It was fees collected from my classmates for some school activity and I was asked to keep the money for the week. That Saturday I happened to go to a bookstore and found a book I liked there. I bought the book with the money, thinking that I would ask my parents to pay it back as soon as I got home. When I told them what I had done, my father was very angry. He said that I had "embezzled" public funds. This was the only time my father got furious with me.

You described your mother as "a virtuous wife and a good mother," I wouldn't use the same characterization for my mother, even though she was a loving mother and a devoted wife. There was something special about my mother. From childhood on she repeatedly said this to me: "as a woman, you must strive hard to stand tall" (做女人要争气 / *zuo nüren yao zhengqi*). At the time I was too young to understand what she meant, but the words were engraved in my mind. Back then we were treated in gender-neutral ways and nobody had said anything about how to be a woman. So those words stuck out. I now realize my mother had a strong sense about being a woman. Through her own experiences she knew only too well life was full of adversities for a woman, but she still wanted me to exert myself and sowed the seed in me when I was only a little girl.

Sometimes at the dinner table my mother would reminisce about the difficulties women cadres with children faced in Yan'an during wartime. How hard, for instance, they had to look for a piece of cloth for their kids and then taught themselves how to sew, as many of them had come from well-to-do families and had never sewed before. My mother often lent a hand to her friends. Daily life details such as this gave me a somewhat different picture about women's experience in Yan'an from those glossed descriptions in books.

My parents worked at the same department in Xinhua where my father was the deputy head and my mother an ordinary editor. My mother disliked this arrangement. At home my parents were equal—that was my impression. My father never acted as a boss and my parents always consulted with each other and made decisions together. If in your family your father was the center, I came to realize as I grew older that in my family the pillar was my mother.

My mother also influenced me in another important way. She often told me, "Don't bother to learn 'woman's work.'" So I knew nothing about sewing, knitting, and stuff like that. I only learned how to cook after I got married.

MA: Same here. As a small girl I always stayed away from household chores. My two brothers did a lot more. My parents never said that I should learn to do these things because I was a girl.

YE: My mother did little housework herself, thanks to Auntie Ma, the live-in domestic helper in our home. Having domestic helpers was common in communist cadres' households, so that the wives could devote themselves more fully to work. Auntie Ma joined our family when I was six and stayed with us for more than 20 years. She was widowed at a young age and it was the local custom for widows in her region to seek work in Beijing. She had "liberated feet," that is, feet that used to be bound but later were let go. They were able to grow back a bit but the shape was permanently altered. I often heard her complaining how difficult it was to find shoes that would fit.

MA: I also remember Aunt Qiu, our domestic helper, for her small feet. Every night before going to bed she would wash her feet in hot water in a basin. Since we shared the same bedroom, I often sat on a stool watching. I was able to see her feet up close and noticed that besides the big toes, all the other toes were pressed under. When she put her feet in the hot water, she would make a certain sound as if she were groaning. I could tell that she felt relieved. She told me her feet ached at the end of the day and the hot water helped reduce the pain. I learned what the old society was about through Aunt Qiu's bound feet.

YE: Auntie Ma came from the same region as my mother and they got along very well. She retired in the early 1980s from our home and went back to live with her daughter in rural Hebei. After my mother developed Alzheimer's disease, she would come to Beijing for a few months every year to keep my mother company. Rapidly losing her memory, my mother sometimes failed to even recognize us, but she always trustingly followed Auntie Ma. One thing my mother relished in her old age was dancing *yangge* (秧歌), a peasant folk dance popular in Yan'an. She always invited Auntie Ma to join her and together they had a lot of fun. Seeing two white-haired women, one crippled and the other bound footed, dancing *yangge*, which required a lot of body movement, I felt like both laughing and crying.

MA: Like your auntie, Aunt Qiu was also widowed at a young age. She came to our family when my little elder brother and I were in elementary school and she left when we started secondary school. The meals Aunt Qiu cooked tasted so delicious. She always kept our home clean and in good order. Because of this, she did not let me bring friends to play. They could only come when she was not around. When they heard her coming, they would hide under a bed and she would use a big broom to get them out. We were all scared of her. I thought she was too harsh with my friends and complained to my father a number of times. But he never did anything. Aunt Qiu addressed my parents as "comrade." Prior to 1949 domestic helpers used terms such as "*laoye*" (master) and "*taitai*" (madam) for their employers. I believe in general domestic helpers enjoyed more respect and higher status after 1949.

YE: It probably had some truth in it, but it also depended on individual families. There was a neighborhood committee in the Xinhua compound. The people serving on the committee were some Xinhua employees' wives and a few domestic helpers, including an elderly lady I called "big aunty" who worked for our next-door neighbor. In the eye of a child, the committee representatives enjoyed lots of authority. One thing the committee did periodically was to hold sanitation contests among the households in the compound. Those that met the sanitary standard would get a little red flag posted on their units' doors. Big aunty took her responsibility very seriously. Thanks to the committee she had a public role to play and I guess that gave her greater self-respect.

* * *

The World of Compounds

These days an itinerary for foreign visitors to Beijing often includes a tour of "hutong" (胡同) or alleyways where "siheyuan" (squared dwelling, a courtyard with one-story houses on its four sides) are located. What often misses a visitor's attention is another Beijing, embodied by numerous "dayuan" (大院 / da-yuan, compounds) scattered all over the city, hidden in enclosed walls.

Dayuan refers to a compound that can contain both work and residential quarters of a danwei (work unit), be it a government agency, a military organization, or a state enterprise. The inhabitants are the employees of a given work unit. As a form of material culture, it only appeared in large scale after the founding of the PRC in 1949, especially in major cities where there was a concentration of government organizations. As many as hundreds or even thousands of people could live in the same compound, forming a society of its own with little interaction with the folksier life in the alleyways surrounding it. The emergence of dayuan represented the state's endeavor to reconstruct everyday life in the "new society" and to maintain, to a certain extent, the communal lifestyle characteristic of the war period in communist-run base areas. It also reflected a time of material scarcity and shortage of service. Typically, a big compound would run a canteen, a general store, a barbershop, and a public bathhouse to meet the needs of its inhabitants.

Dayuan bespoke a new stratification system in Chinese society. In general, only middle- and lower-ranking employees lived in dayuan. High cadres often had their own single-family residences elsewhere.

In today's China, dayuan still exists in major urban centers, but the communal feature it used to embody has withered. With the development of a market economy, it's no longer necessary for dayuan to provide essential services. A way of life has largely disappeared.

YE: I grew up in Xinhua compound in downtown Beijing. The entire compound occupied more than 70 *mu* of land (about 12 acres). It was divided into work and residential areas. When I was small there was no armed security force guarding the work area as there is today. We children could roam about the entire territory. We often played the game "looking for the arrow," a sort of hide-and-seek between two groups of kids. It allowed us to explore every corner of the compound. Some areas were no-man's-land and it was scary to find oneself there alone.

The compound feels like a big village to me every time I go back for a visit from America. Just as peasants dwell in the same village for all their lives, Xinhua people have lived together for as long as I can remember. They might have moved into new and better-equipped buildings, but they haven't moved out of the compound. Now the compound has become very crowded. Almost every inch of land has been utilized for office or apartment buildings. No more obscure corners for children to play "looking for the arrow."

Most of the people now are living in the high-rises built since the 1980s. There is not much interaction between the neighbors except a brief "hello" in the elevator. Children living next door don't play together. After school they stay at home watching TV and playing computer games by themselves. Perhaps I am being nostalgic, but I miss the days when kids could mingle easily. The building where my family lived during the 1950s and early 1960s helped facilitate a sense of community. Constructed in the mid-1950s, it was a four-story building with long and wide hallway on every floor. On both sides of the hallway were two- or three-bedroom units, each with a toilet but no kitchen. The families on the same floor—there were about six or seven units—shared a common kitchen, which was large enough for each household to maintain a coal burning stove, a cabinet, and a small table. The kitchen also served as a common room for neighbors to chat and exchange news although most of the time it was the domain of the domestic helpers. It was not easy to keep family secrets from the neighbors.

I don't know how the adults felt about the closeness of the living arrangement. With hindsight I realize they might not have liked it that much, especially when there was a political campaign going on. After a criticism meeting in the office, they would have wanted to avoid their colleagues in the living quarter and privacy would have been desirable. But for us kids who had little sense of the adult world, this living arrangement was great. Girls tended to stay inside with friends playing house and other domestic games, while boys formed gangs and often ran wild outside fighting in their war games. I don't remember ever hearing any complaints from adults about the boys' behavior. Perhaps it was because all the leaders at Xinhua had children in this age group. When it was dinnertime, you would hear a kid's name being called loudly by a mother or more likely an auntie to go home. Parents knew their children were somewhere in the compound with friends and there was no need to worry.

Without leaving the compound, one could get almost every type of service. The service was not free but it was cheaper than what would have been charged outside. Besides, you also didn't have to wait in long lines. My parents deposited their money at the compound bank and mailed their letters in the compound post office. When I didn't feel well I would go to the compound clinic. My parents joined a medical program for children so I didn't need to bring any cash with me. I knew every doctor and nurse there and would try to avoid the ones with a poor reputation.

My favorite places were the library and the auditorium. I spent a lot of time in the library, doing homework in the reading room and browsing the many journals and newspapers on the shelves. They came from every province in China and even countries like the Soviet Union and Hungary. I was also able to borrow books from the library, with my mother's card. The auditorium was another memorable place. Almost every Saturday evening a film was shown there free for Xinhua residents. To see a new film with my girl friends was the highlight of the week. Over the years I saw many feature films made both in China and abroad.

MA: There wasn't an auditorium in the compound where we lived. As a matter of fact, most of the facilities you describe didn't exist in ours except for a canteen. We lived in a compound that belonged to my father's work unit. It was a small, strictly residential compound with only four multistory redbrick buildings. The offices of the ministry were elsewhere. Located within a *hutong*, our compound looked like "a crane standing among chickens." We shopped in the nearby *hutong* and streets because there were no stores in our compound.

Children in the compound also played together. I always went to a girl's home. She had a very pretty elder sister who was an actress. I liked to go to their home just to see the sister. I also noticed another good-looking girl in our compound. Her eyebrows were long and her eyes were deep and large. She and my brother eventually fell in love and she is now my sister-in-law. I used to call her "gypsy girl" behind her back because I thought she looked like a foreigner. I admired beautiful people. My father once observed that "whenever you see a pretty woman you cannot take your eye off her."

In our compound it was hard to keep secrets. The family living next to us had several children. The father was a well-respected Red Army veteran. All his children were doing well except the youngest one, a daughter. She was pretty and liked to dress differently from other girls. She always wore strikingly bright colors and her clothes were tailored to fit her body. By then a simple lifestyle was being promoted as proletarian, so people like her were seen as pursuing a decadent bourgeois way of life. Later she spent sometime in a reform center for delinquent adolescents. Rumor had it that she had gotten into trouble because of "loose behavior." When she came back from the reform center she moved out of her parents' apartment and lived by herself in a small room facing the windows of our apartment. I was curious about her and would sometimes stand by the window to peep, but her door and windows were always shut tight and she never spoke to any neighbors. She still dressed in a manner that provoked frowns. Neighbors remarked in low voices, "Look at her. How disgusting!" Everybody's behavior was under public scrutiny. This was a characteristic of compound life.

I also remember some old residents such as a retired man who lived in our building. He had participated in the Long March and therefore was a big hero in our eyes. He regularly cleaned the banisters of the staircase in our building. Once I watched him doing it: he walked very slowly, one step at a time, carefully dusting the banisters. He did it voluntarily, which made me respect him even more.

The best known person in our compound was Uncle Li who worked at the reception room. His job also included cleaning the yard and delivering telephone messages. Since most residents in the compound didn't have telephones at home, the phone in the reception room was very busy. Uncle Li's trademark was his resounding voice. Our compound had almost 200 households and Uncle Li knew every family by heart. When a phone call came for someone, he would walk to the right building and call up to the person. Every word was clearly pronounced and the sound echoed throughout the entire compound.

Uncle Li didn't get married until his sixties. When the news came out everyone felt happy for him. Many people bought presents. After his marriage his salary was no longer sufficient. Somebody suggested that each family add one or two *jiao* (ten *fen* makes one *jiao*) to their monthly fee for Uncle Li's cleaning. People agreed that it would be very little for each family but could make a big difference for Uncle Li.

Since his small two-room residence was just opposite our apartment, my family had an especially close relationship with Uncle Li. Every time I went out I had to pass his home and I must have greeted him thousands of times. In the early 1980s my family purchased a refrigerator, a rarity at the time. One day Uncle Li asked my parents if he could put a fish in our freezer. Of course he could, my parents said. The fish was sitting in the freezer for a long time, perhaps over two months. One day my big elder brother said that Uncle Li must have forgotten his fish and we should remind him. My father replied, "No, he didn't forget. He is saving it for a special occasion. Let's leave it there." My father was right: Uncle Li finally came to get his fish one day.

YE: Were cadres expected to respect working-class people more in those days? I remember a wall poster (大字报/ *dazibao*) by the chefs at Xinhua canteen. It was posted in an area where people put wall posters to voice their grievances and draw attention to issues of public concern. This particular poster criticized a cadre for defending his son who had been rude to the chefs. Many people wrote in response to criticize the cadre. In the end that man had to apologize. I remember this incident well because I disliked his son very much. He was a spoiled brat.

Hearing you talk about Uncle Li, I'm reminded of a man in our compound. His last name was Guan. Behind his back, we kids called him "Old Guan," which wasn't very respectful. Whenever there was a show in the auditorium that was not open to us children, like the screening of a *neibu*[3] (内部) movie, Old Guan would guard the gate. We wanted very much to sneak into the auditorium but the fierce look on his face scared us away. In his old age he became half paralyzed by a stroke. When I went back to Beijing to visit my family I sometimes saw him slowly dragging his body across the compound. I would watch him from afar and wonder if I should go up to say hello. I was not sure if he still remembered me as one of the naughty kids in front of the auditorium making trouble for him.

MA: Your playmates all seemed to be kids from Xinhua. Our compound was located in an alleyway and I went to school in another alleyway, so many of my friends were from *hutong*. After school we often played together. I visited some of my friends' homes and was surprised to see how small and crowded they were. The ceilings were low and the rooms were dark. There was no indoor plumbing or toilets.

A different kind of family also lived in *hutong*. Once I was invited to visit a classmate's home. The girl warned me beforehand not to speak in a loud voice. Her family resided in a well-maintained large courtyard house with all the modern facilities. The rooms were tall and spacious, furnished with hardwood furniture in traditional style. I watched my every move and was nervous that I might break something. In one room I saw an elderly lady sitting straight in an elegant chair. She was probably my friend's grandmother. Few old ladies dressed so well those days. She made me think of the wicked landlord's mother in a movie I'd seen. I felt ill at ease and didn't stay long.

YE: I was not as familiar like you with life in *hutong*. Most of my knowledge about alleyways came from my third (maternal) uncle's home, which was in a typical courtyard in western Beijing. Three other families shared my uncle's courtyard housing. As the landlord, my uncle's family occupied the rooms facing the south, the best side, and the tenant families rented rooms on the other three sides. A huge porcelain fish jar stood in the center of the spacious open yard. I always liked to watch the gold fish swimming. Near my uncle's section there stood two date trees. Every autumn my brother and I waited anxiously for the sweet and crispy dates from the trees. My uncle planted some vegetables and flowers in his backyard. It felt as if it were in the countryside rather than in the middle of downtown Beijing.

My uncle's courtyard had a different atmosphere from the Xinhua compound. The neighbors greeted each other courteously in accordance with traditional etiquette, unlike in the compound where everybody was supposed to be a fellow comrade. I was not sure if I behaved properly in their eyes.

*   *   *

"Study Hard and Make Progress Everyday"

We began elementary school at the age of seven and, unlike in the United States, we stayed with the same class until graduation. Each class, or ban jiti (class collective), was assigned a classroom where every student had a desk and chair. This arrangement gave the children a sense of "place," both literally and figuratively. With the large size of a class (usually with over 45 students), it was hardly possible for the homeroom teacher to pay sufficient attention to each child. This situation made self-governance by the students necessary.

Beginning at the third grade, a class would simultaneously become a Young Pioneers' company. A children's organization under the leadership of the Communist Party, a Young Pioneers organization contains three levels of order: brigade (大队 / dadui), company (中队 / zhongdui), and platoon (小队 / xiaodui). I still believe that back in the 1950s and part of the 1960s, the Young Pioneers, though undoubtedly following the political instruction of the Communist Party, nonetheless provided a platform where children learned to take charge of their own affairs. Many acquired social and organizational skills that would be beneficial to their future lives in numerous ways. In the case of my class, a large number of Young Pioneers events were initiated by my classmates when we reached the sixth grade. The activities fell into two basic categories: having fun and doing good deeds (such as helping needy people), not that much different from what the Boy & Girl Scouts did. We elected the leaders at the company and platoon levels and it was an honor to be trusted by one's fellow students.

MA: When I stepped into the campus of my elementary school in September, 1958, I was immediately drawn to the eight big characters in bright red color on a white screen wall: "study hard and make progress every-day" (好好学习, 天天向上), written in Chairman Mao's handwriting style. These were the words he said to us children. The eight words captured my spirit at the time—earnest and upbeat. I had looked forward to my first day of school as if it were a holiday. I always tried to be the best. I studied very hard and always got good grades. One semester we had seven math tests in a short run and I didn't lose a single point. I felt so good about myself that I remarked to a classmate, "How come I have never received a 4 (an equivalent to a B)? I'd love to know how it feels to get one." Stupidly I repeated the same words to my father. He was not impressed and said to me, "You're too arro-gant!" Striving for excellence was a characteristic of our generation. We acquired it not because of the pressure to pass school entrance examinations but because we just wanted to be good students.

YE: But to go to a good secondary school you needed to pass the entrance examination with high scores, and that meant pressure. We usually didn't feel it until close to the exam year.

MA: I was not the only student who refused to accept second best. On the day when there was a contest for personal hygiene, a girl in my class forgot to cut her nails, so she bit off the nails to avoid getting a low point. Another time the same girl saw a "2" (D) on her report card. Without looking at it carefully, she thought that she had failed a test and began to cry. It only occurred to her later that the "2" meant two sick days. I was just like her. We took turns cleaning our classroom every morning. One day my group was on duty. That morning I got up very early and walked to school when it was still dark. Imagine a little girl doing that by herself! I don't understand why I was not scared then and why my parents didn't object to what I was doing. As soon as the school gate was open, I rushed into the classroom and started the cleaning. By the time the rest of my group arrived, the job was already done.

One nice memory I have of my elementary school is the spring field trip. Long before the event we started to talk about it with excitement. The most important question was what food to bring. There was an unspoken competition among us and nobody wanted to lose face. I always brought Western style bread, which was considered a treat in those days. What to wear also required careful thinking as I wished to look my best for the occasion. Trees had started turning green and flowers were in blossom. I wanted to match the beautiful colors in nature. After the trip we often wrote a composition for our Chinese class, and this gave me another opportunity to excel. I kept a notebook in which I had collected many fancy adjectives. Now it was time to use them. When the teacher returned our compositions, she usually selected the best to read to the class. As I expected, mine was chosen. This put a nice final touch to our spring outing.

YE: I also have fond memories of our spring field trips. The two places we frequented over the years were the Beijing Zoo and the Summer Palace. I also remember the part "food" played in these trips. A boiled egg was what the majority of the people would bring, to go with bread or homemade steamed bun. Sausages would be a nice addition. My memory of one classmate is always associated with the nice sausages he brought to the spring trip.

MA: One thing I like about this period is that if you had talent in some area you would be able to develop it. Those who loved to sing could join the chorus in the municipal children's palace. Those fascinated with science could sign up for a science club at a district children's center, and so on. When I was in the fourth grade the local After School Athletic Training Center was recruiting students. I was recommended by the physical education teacher to go. I wanted to learn swimming but the coach was absent that day. I stood there by myself and didn't know what to do. A young woman came by. She looked me up and down and asked if I would like to try gymnastics. I said yes. Looking back I see it was my good fortune that the swimming coach didn't show up that day. Gymnastics suited me much better. It made me appreciate the beauty of body movement. After three years of practice, I received a national certificate as a qualified gymnast.

My father was not happy when I took up gymnastics. He especially disliked my coach and thought she looked ostentatiously "foreign." When she walked, she carried her body in such a way that some people would stop to admire while others would frown. In my father's eyes her posture was definitely not proletarian. But I liked her graceful style. She was a devoted teacher, both strict and caring. When class got out late she would ride me to the bus stop on her bicycle. Once I was sitting on the rear seat of her bike. In order not to fall, I was holding her waist. Suddenly, the road became bumpy and I accidentally touched her breast. And I reacted like, "Wow, it is so soft." For the first time in my life I had some sense of a woman's body.

After a couple of years, I stopped practicing gymnastics. Then something else caught my fancy. One winter I went to Beihai Park and found that the whole lake had become a huge ice-skating rink. One young woman stood out as a particularly good skater. Quite a few men had stopped skating to watch her. I thought to myself, "With my training as a gymnast I can easily become a good skater." I asked my father to buy me a pair of skates. I pleaded and begged, but his answer always was a stern "no." I asked why and he said skating was a bourgeois sport. Many people at the skating rink wore woolen hats, long scarves, and tight woolen sweaters that showed their figures. This image disgusted my father. When I was in junior high, I was almost admitted to a professional dance school—as I only failed the final round of tests. But even if I had passed, my father would not have let me go. In his view things like dancing and skating were self-indulgent bourgeois pursuits.

YE: Sounds like you had great after-school activities. But I'd still like to know more about your regular school class and your schoolteachers.

MA: There wasn't that much that really stands out in my memory either about my class or any of the teachers.

YE: Well, I really liked my class a lot and have many pleasant memories about it.

MA: Were you a student cadre?

YE: No. The highest position I ever held was a deputy platoon leader in the Young Pioneers, the lowest officer in the organization. I felt embarrassed to wear the armband with only one red stroke on it.[4]

MA: Mine had three strokes.

YE: So you were a brigade leader, a big cadre. In my school, brigade leaders were celebrities and were admired by other students.

I went to the No.2 Experimental Elementary School of Beijing, a very good school with a long history. It was only ten-minute walk from the Xinhua compound. I began my school in 1957. To be admitted into the school, one needed to take a competitive entrance examination. I don't remember the content of the exam, but my father remembers that I cried after taking the exam. It must have been nerve-racking for a kid to take her first exam.

My school was run by two elderly ladies. The principal was prominent in the field of elementary-school education and served as a member of the National People's Congress. Since she had to attend a lot of meetings outside the school, the vice principal handled everyday business. She was a short, energetic woman. The two ladies apparently belonged to an earlier generation of career women in China. I doubt if they were Communist Party members, but they seemed to have decision-making power and enjoyed high respect from both faculty and students.

I remember my first-grade homeroom teacher[5] well. She was a tall plump woman in her forties. The first day of school she said something that has stayed with me until today: "Once somebody becomes your teacher, even if it's only for one day, the person remains a parent figure for the rest of your life" (一日为师，终身为父 / yi ri wei shi zhong shen wei fu). Because of the rude attitude many people in our generation displayed toward their teachers during the Cultural Revolution, I heard people say that we had never been taught to respect teachers. This was not true.

During the six years of elementary school homeroom teachers for my class changed several times, but we pupils stayed together throughout the entire period. I liked it this way because it gave me a sense of belonging. Our class went through some rough phases. It was particularly bad when we entered the fourth grade. Paper airplanes sailed across the classroom during teachers' lecturing. Some boys were so naughty that they made the homeroom teacher, a young woman, cry many times. Finally in our fifth year, Teacher Wu came and things began to turn around. Our class evolved into a cohesive unit and a genuine *ban jiti* (class collective). We even composed a class poem with the help of Teacher Wu that wove the stories of many classmates together. At the graduation time, we exchanged photos and addresses and vowed that we would have a class reunion every year. My classmates have kept this promise for many years.

As a Young Pioneer company, our class was divided into three platoons, each with about 15 members. In my opinion the real vitality of my class lay in the platoons. The platoon leaders, elected annually, were people with real power, since most of the activities were conducted at this level. The three platoons competed with each other in many activities. Each platoon was assigned a space on the wall for a monthly wallpaper (墙报 / qiangbao).

The content of the paper was kept as a top secret before each issue came out. My platoon often went to a classmate's home after school to work on the paper. I was responsible for the artistic design. Once I borrowed ideas from the window designs in the Summer Palace. Some windows there were shaped like a peach, a book, or a fan, and so on. I decorated our wallpaper with these different shapes and it looked really cute.

There was much I loved about my school, but there was also something that made me feel uncomfortable. Because of my school's reputation, it attracted quite a number of children of the social and political elite, either high ranking communist cadres or nonparty people holding high positions in the government. One girl in my class was the daughter of a vice premier of the State Council. In the other three classes of our grade, there were the daughter of another vice premier, the son of a vice chairman of the National People's Congress, and the daughter of a vice president of the state. The same was true with other grades. Three of Liu Shaoqi's (the president of China) children attended my school.

In such an environment, students were sensitive to the ranks of the parents. Since officials above certain rank rode in cars provided by the state, a favorite topic among the boys in my class was cars. They knew very well which rank was supposed to ride in what car. Listening to their "car talk" made me aware that my parents were just ordinary cadres. I felt inferior. This uneasy feeling followed me throughout my elementry school years.

MA: Was there any discrimination at school?

YE: Not from the school administration or any teachers. But you tended to take what your peers said to heart. Social hierarchy was a reality in my school. Every time there was a parent–teacher conference some parents would arrive with secretaries and bodyguards. They greeted each other as if they were at a Central Party Committee meeting. Parked cars formed a long line in the alleyway outside the school. My father simply walked to the school from the Xinhua compound. How I wished he would also come by car.

MA: Did the high-cadre children enjoy any privilege?

YE: The only case I can recall was a special treatment given to the four children of one vice premier. They had the use of a room next to the school gate to have their lunch brought to them each day by their "auntie" from home.

In this rather elitist environment, we were fortunate to have Teacher Wu as our homeroom teacher. He came from a peasant family but was not ashamed of his rural origin. He spoke with a rural Hebei accent and dressed like a village schoolteacher. His country style was out of tune with an elite urban school, but it didn't seem to bother him. Before long he won our respect because he treated us with respect. He talked to us like a friend or a big brother and this made us feel we were grown-ups. He liked to share with us his thoughts about the books and articles he'd read or his observations of social problems, especially when he saw something he thought was unjust.

We learned that his family was only able to support one child's education so his sister had sacrificed her opportunity for his sake. He talked about this to us a number of times. Later I realized that he had a purpose in telling us about his family. He wanted us urban, generally privileged kids to get a sense of how people in other situations lived.

One thing he said has left a deep impression on many of us. That day we went to Beihai Park—our favorite park—to hold our company Young Pioneers Day. Teacher Wu was with us. The theme of the day was to talk about what we wanted to be when we grew up. In those days we were always encouraged to imagine our future. We found a quiet corner in the scenic park, sat in a circle, and took turns speaking. Scientists, engineers, and writers were some of the more common career goals. One girl wanted to become a horticulturist so that she could graft tomato plants upon potatoes to produce a new type of vegetable. The idea was not original—more than one science books we'd read had mentioned it—but to hear it articulated by a classmate still impressed us. I didn't know what to be. Somebody suggested that since I liked to draw, why not become an artist. So my goal was to be an artist. In the end we all aspired to be somebody. Afterward we took a trolley back to school. Still carried away by the great prospects we envisioned for ourselves, we continued to talk with excitement. Suddenly somebody noticed that Teacher Wu had remained silent all this time and asked him why. He replied, "Nobody wants to be a peasant."

MA: He said that?

YE: Yes. He must have felt sad that none of his students even thought about the rural people. Of course, at the time none of us would imagine in our wildest dreams that some day most of us would become peasants and live for years in the countryside.

As a Chinese language teacher, he did one thing that all of us still cherish. In our sixth grade, he began to introduce us to classical Chinese poems that were not in the curriculum. We read poems by such timeless poets as Du Fu, Su Dongpo, and Xin Qiji.[6] To make the learning fun, each poem we studied for the week was accompanied by a drawing done by a student. The drawing was posted on the wall and it gave us an opportunity to comment and critique. We liked to argue whether the drawing captured the spirit of the poem as we understood. For a while we steeped ourselves in the magnificent world of classical Chinese poetry, competing with each other to see who could recite more. It was a wonderful experience.

Another memorable event in our sixth grade was a calligraphy contest. Teacher Wu invited Teacher Jia, our calligraphy teacher, to be the judge. A man in his sixties, Teacher Jia carried himself like a scholar from the old days. It was not a real calligraphy contest in the traditional way, since we used ink pens and regular paper instead of fur brushes and rice paper. Each of us copied the same essay picked up by Teacher Wu from our Chinese textbook and our handwriting was ranked by Teacher Jia. The essay was written by the famous writer Ba Jin, entitled "The Stars in the Sky" ("繁星" / *fan xing*). It begins this way, "I love the moon-lit night, but I also love the stars that fill the sky . . . It makes me feel I'm in mother's bosom." If writings have "colors," this piece is a serene dark blue. We all fell in love with the essay. For a while after the calligraphy contest we tried to apply the sentence pattern "I love . . . but I also love . . . " whenever we could. A student wrote a composition emulating the entire essay. Previously I had only noticed this boy's sloppy demeanor, but his writing completely changed my view of him.

* * *

"The Three Difficult Years"

The "three difficult years" refers to the period from 1959 to 1961, when the impact of the disastrous Great Leap Forward was widely felt, most keenly in the form of food shortage. The famine led to an enormously high death toll among the rural population. Life in urban China was also affected, though not as badly. Even for people like Ma Xiaodong and me whose families enjoyed certain privileges in terms of food supply, hunger was not an unfamiliar sensation.

MA: I clearly remember this period during my elementary-school years. One day I was eating a piece of corn bread on my way to school. I cannot forget the eyes of some people in the street who stared at my corn bread. I was terrified. Another time I ran into a beggar, a man in his thirties. He walked directly up to me and asked for food. I did not have any food with me and didn't know what to say. I was both scared and confused. Why did people beg for food? This was not supposed to happen in the new society.

Among my classmates, there was a girl named Fan Lili. After school I often played with her. She lived in an alleyway and her family was probably working class. When we were together one day, she cried and said that she felt hungry all the time. Every day her mother would cook a big pot of porridge. She wouldn't let the family eat it until the porridge cooled down and the liquid turned into solid mass. It felt as if one were eating a lot, but Fan Lili said her stomach would soon feel empty again. The family ate porridge this way three times a day.

Food also dominated my mind. My mouth would water whenever I saw a steamed bun or a pancake. Aunt Qiu was not with us around this time so my little elder brother and I ate our meals in the compound canteen. One evening my father found us lying in bed, looking listless. He asked if we had eaten supper. I said, "Not really," because we had spent the supper meal tickets on that day's lunch. But we did eat something for supper—we ate ginger. My father asked if the ginger was too spicy. I said, "No, it was not spicy. It was sweet." Hearing this, my father's eyes turned red. He must have realized that I was making the best of an inadequate supper. Still, I didn't have to eat porridge every day like Fan Lili.

Every food item was rationed: grain, cooking oil, sugar, eggs, meat, vegetables, you name it, and there were few fresh fruits on the market. One day some people came to our compound to sell peaches, one peach per family. I was playing outside in the compound when they came. Hearing the news I burst into my home to report it to my parents. My father still remembers the excitement on my face after all these years. One peach might sound like very little, but my father later told me that his ministry had managed to get the peaches for its employees and their families. So it would not be available for families like Fan Lili's.

There were other more significant privileges enjoyed by cadres and their families. Cadres above certain ranks were provided with extra sugar, cooking oil, eggs, and meat.[7] These commodities were sold at a special store that required a card to enter. I remember buying these food items for my family. I waved the card to the guards at the gate and they nodded politely to let me in. When I left the store with food, my feeling toward the people in the streets was like, "See, I have something you don't have." Two *jin* (1 *jin* equals to 1.1 pounds) of meat and one *jin* of sugar per month are nothing by today's standards, but they made a big difference then.

YE: My family also enjoyed some privileges. Because of the food shortage, many urban dwellers contracted edema due to malnutrition. I saw quite a few cases at the Xinhua clinic. The way to tell was to press a person's leg. If a deep hollow appeared, this was a sure sign. The doctor would prescribe a certain amount of soybeans for the patient. No medicine was needed.

Did you ever have artificial meat? The Xinhua canteen once sold dishes made of it. It looked red and white just like pork, but it tasted like candle wax. I'm not sure if it even contained soybeans.

MA: Speaking of meat, I remember an incident during this period. One day my mother announced that she would cook us a pork dish. Anticipating a good meal, we all got excited. But the meat was overcooked and hardly edible. My mother was so upset that she cried, blaming herself for an "unforgivable" mistake. My father tried to comfort her. At moments like this he was very understanding. My mother had never cried in front of us so I remember the scene very well.

YE: This period tested the strength of a family. A person's grain ration was determined by age, sex, and occupation. Some families applied the public calculations to their private dining tables. Children were given less food because of their lower ration. This happened to some kids I knew in the Xinhua compound, but my family had none of it. The three adults, my father, mother, and auntie, always put my brother and me first. They said we needed nutrition to grow.

Even so, like you I was obsessed with food. At school food was a constant topic. A classmate shared with us his discovery of haw balls. They were made of hawthorn fruits with a sour–sweet taste and could be purchased at any Chinese medicine store. We all rushed to buy them. But the more we ate the hungrier we became since the haw balls were supposed to stimulate appetite.

MA: I once did something crazy. I asked my mother if I could have as many eggs as I wanted. My mother agreed. I ended up eating seven eggs and still didn't feel full. But my mother said, "That's it." I only realized later that seven eggs probably made up a considerable portion of my family's monthly ration. But nobody said a word to me that day about my greediness, not even my little elder brother.

YE: Speaking of eggs, I'm reminded of our hen. Because of the shortage of food, Xinhua allowed its employees to raise chickens for eggs and meat. Almost every family I knew had a hen or two. They were kept in a long row of chicken coops built along the backside of our building. My family had a white Leghorn. She started laying eggs right after the Spring Festival and remained productive for much of the year. I liked to fetch the freshly laid eggs. Holding a warm egg in my hand gave me a nice sensation. Years later when I was a sent-down youth, every time I received a letter from home I felt as if I were holding a warm egg. The white Leghorn was like my pet and I even wrote an essay about her for my Chinese composition class. Her eggs provided the necessary nutrition for my newborn younger sister. She was a hero in my family.

But her end came in an abrupt way. One day we heard that no more chicken raising was allowed in the compound. The rumor had it that it was because the head of Xinhua had slipped on some chicken droppings inside his apartment building and was furious. We had to give our Leghorn away to a relative. It made me sad.

*　　*　　*

The Dark Shadow

The history of the PRC in the 1950s and 1960s was punctuated by political campaigns. Prior to the Cultural Revolution, "Anti-rightist Campaign" of 1957–1958 was the most notorious and damaging. It resulted in the persecution of approximately half a million people, primarily intellectuals and many the best and brightest in the Chinese society. They had responded to the CCP's invitation to criticize its policies only to find that they were caught in a political scheme against "anti-party reactionaries." Many lost their jobs and were sent to remote labor camps if not downright prisons. Their families often suffered political discrimination. Political campaigns like this comprise a heavy dark page in the PRC's history. As children growing up during this period, how much were we aware of the chilly side of the Chinese reality? While Ma Xiaodong appeared to be unaware of the repression, because of the experiences of some relatives, I had some limited knowledge. What follows is my recollection.

I had relatives on both sides of my parents who suffered in 1957 as rightists: my third and fifth uncles on my father's side and my third uncle on my mother's. Both my third and fifth paternal uncles were veteran members of the Democratic League, an organization made up of liberal thinking Western-educated intellectuals.[8] After 1949, my third uncle Ye Duyi was appointed to a high-level post in the Chinese People's Political Consultative Conference, a prestigious position for a non-CCP person. In his youth my fifth uncle Ye Duzhuang was the most radical of all the brothers. His left-leaning thinking greatly influenced my father, his younger brother. Trained as an agronomist in both China and Japan, he worked at the Academy of Agricultural Science after 1949. My third maternal uncle, Bai Jingyang, taught Chinese language and literature in a reputable secondary school in Beijing. In his youth he had studied in Japan and was well versed in classical Chinese philosophy and literature. He was my mother's only surviving sibling, since my first and second uncles both lost their lives during the Sino-Japanese War.

All my uncles' lives were dramatically altered by the Anti-rightist Campaign. My third paternal uncle lost his esteemed job and had to get by with a much reduced salary. Yet he fared better than my fifth uncle, who was accused of being an American spy on top of being a rightist, and was sentenced to ten years' imprisonment on totally groundless charges. My third maternal uncle, meanwhile, lost his teaching job and was sent to do manual labor on a tree farm in the suburbs of Beijing. His family had to sell his collection of antiques and rare paintings to make ends meet.

I must have had some awareness of the Anti-rightist Campaign as it was unfolding. Otherwise why was I so scared when I saw my third paternal uncle appear in a newsreel in the summer of 1957? I left the Xinhua auditorium right away, dragging my brother along. On the screen my uncle was speaking at a meeting. He wore a black short-sleeved shirt and had a Chinese-style fan in his hand. Everything looked normal. But somehow I knew things were not right. That meeting was apparently the occasion when my uncle spoke up "to attack the party and the government." He was eventually labeled an important member of the Zhang-Luo Anti-Party Alliance, the most infamous reactionary clique "dug up" during the Anti-rightist Campaign.[9]

In the ensuing weeks after I saw my uncle on screen, whenever there was a jeep entering the Xinhua compound, I thought it had taken my uncle to the auditorium for a denunciation meeting. I had seen people taken this way to Xinhua by armed police. Once a meeting was held in the auditorium to condemn a man accused of peeping at women bathing. Children were not allowed to get near the auditorium when such meetings were held, but I saw the man arriving in a green police jeep. It was totally unlikely for this to happen to my uncle, if only because he was not a Xinhua employee. But still I was scared. For the first time in my life I had a taste of fear. It was like a black shadow hanging over an otherwise bright sky. I was barely seven that summer. I don't recall how I learned about my uncle's situation. I must have overheard something from my parents.

I often wonder how the sufferings of their brothers impacted my parents. It would be horrible for me if my brother and sister were being unfairly accused while I was not able to help them. I have no idea what my parents had to say to their party organization, but at home they never said a word about "drawing a line." My family maintained close relationships with all those politically troubled relatives. My fifth uncle's three daughters played with us all the time and often slept over. If anything, my brother and I were closer to them than other cousins. I knew their father was not around and something terrible had happened to him. From time to time, an aunt would come to see my parents. If they shut the door tight and talked in low voices inside, chances were she had brought news about my fifth uncle. He chose to keep correspondence with this sister among his siblings because she was only a housewife. It wouldn't cause her as much trouble to have contact with a brother imprisoned on counter-revolutionary charges. At one point my father tried to help my uncle clear his name. For this he suffered badly during the Cultural Revolution.

My maternal third uncle's political misfortune left his family with financial hardships. His only son, as it turned out, was also labeled a "rightist" and was sent to a labor camp far away. So the family had almost no source of income. Every month when my mother received her paycheck, she would give some money to my aunt and her grandchildren. She didn't skip once even during the Cultural Revolution. Over the years she also helped other relatives in financial need. My father has observed that in the 1950s and 1960s my mother consistently gave half of her monthly salary to help other people.

In the early 1960s, *Nainai* (my grandfather's first secondary wife) came to stay with us for a few months. She was not my father's own mother, but my parents treated her respectfully and my mother acted as a dutiful daughter-in-law. We were told to observe certain etiquette as well-behaved grandchildren in front of *Nainai*. According to the political classification of the day, *Nainai* was a member of the exploiting class, but nobody cared about political labels in our household. I was impressed by my parents and learned how to treat old people from them.

I often wonder how my mother reconciled her profound humanism with her loyalty to the party. I suspect that she must have had misgivings. I will never know what went through her mind and heart, but I know she was not an unthinking person. Once I accidentally read an entry in my mother's diary, in which she expressed sympathy for Peng Dehuai.[10] Even as a child I knew Peng Dehuai was a "bad guy" who had attacked Chairman Mao's Great Leap Forward policy. I was shocked to read that my mother was thinking differently about Peng, but I knew better than to mention it to anybody.

There were always guests in my home, most of whom had come to see my mother with either personal or political grievances. One man lost his party membership because of a "mistake" he'd made while working abroad. His wife divorced him and most people at Xinhua shunned him. For a while he regularly visited my home. My mother was only an ordinary cadre and not in a position to solve anybody's problem, but she gave people warmth and consolation they failed to get elsewhere. If they came around mealtime, my mother would invite them to eat with us. I was too young to understand these people's situations and I could be rude to them if they stayed too long. My mother was in poor health so I didn't want them to tire her. After I grew older and especially after I experienced the Cultural Revolution, I came to admire not only my mother's humanity but also her political courage.

I will always remember a scene in my third maternal uncle's house. It was when my uncle worked on a tree farm and only occasionally returned to the city. When he was back my mother would go to see him and sometimes she would take me along. My mother and her brother would sit in a corner, talking in soft voices. I couldn't hear what they were saying, but there was something touching about the two adult siblings quietly talking to each other in a dimly lit room.

My "rightist" uncles received rehabilitation in the late 1970s[11] when the country finally came out of the nightmare of the Cultural Revolution. They were in their prime years in 1957. Now they were fragile, old men. More than 20 years of their precious lives were gone. Nothing could compensate for such loss.

My fifth paternal uncle returned to Beijing after being absent for two decades, spending the period first in a prison and then in a labor camp. His wife had died of cancer a few years earlier. On her death bed she expressed the wish to see her husband one last time, but the plea was ignored.

After he finally gained freedom, my fifth uncle was able to accomplish one task that had weighted on him mentally even during his days in prison: to bring about a new edition of Charles Darwin's *The Origin of Species* that he and two other men collaboratively translated into Chinese in the early 1950s. Not quite satisfied with the quality of their work, the three translators decided to produce a new translation. However, it took 39 years to see this wish finally fulfilled, in the early 1990s. My uncle, who was the only person among the three left to do the job and who devoted the remainder of his life to introducing Darwin to China, mused about the enormously long time it had taken for the new edition: "When I finished the job [of editing the new edition], what went through my mind was the ceaseless political movements that happened one after another in the previous decades. If not because of this situation, how could the editing of a book have taken so long?"[12] The fate of a book testified to the predicament of a special intellectual cohort in the second half of twentieth-century China. Among them were my three uncles.

THREE

From Paper Crown to Leather Belt[*]

Revolutionizing the Students

*The years prior to the Cultural Revolution were critical in grooming our generation for the roles we were to play in the ensuing political upheaval. What happened on many secondary-school campuses in Beijing at this time was indicative of an overall ideological hardening in China, signified most clearly by Mao Zedong's September 1962 call to "never forget class struggle." It reflected Mao's perception of a perilous reality both in domestic politics and in international affairs. Domestically, Mao disapproved of what he regarded as ideologically compromising policies, such as retreating from rural collectivization attempted by his lieutenants in the wake of the disastrous Great Leap Forward. He sensed his influence at the party center was being weakened. Internationally, it appeared that Mao believed that the Soviet Union had betrayed the **truth "Marxism"** and had turned "revisionist." The open rift between the two giant socialist countries created great strain and led to serious border tension in the north. Meanwhile, America's escalated military presence in Vietnam posed explicit threat from the south.*

Around this time, an alleged deathbed wish of United States former Secretary of States John Foster Dulles was widely circulated among the Chinese populace. Realizing that it was impossible to corrupt the revolutionary generation of Mao and his comrades, Dulles placed his hope of peaceful evolution to capitalism in China on the "third generation"—who were seen as soft and malleable. That was my generation.

Against this backdrop, Mao raised the issue of training millions of "revolutionary successors" to ensure that China would remain a stronghold of world revolution. It was time for the Chinese youth to get serious, to show Dulles that his wish was bound to shatter. Our generation thus acquired a special responsibility for China's political future. To live up to this expectation, we needed to reform our thinking so that revolutionary ideas would take over our minds. In this context, a "revolutionizing movement" took place on many secondary-school campuses in Beijing. This movement and similar political campaigns amounted to a thought reform that targeted teenagers such as Ma Xiaodong and myself. Books and films played a significant role in the revolutionizing endeavor, offering captivating models for us to emulate.

As young women, what happened to us had a gendered dimension. We shed skirts and blouses to put on loosely fitting pants and jackets. To be a revolutionary implicitly meant to look like a man. Femininity had no place in the all-encompassing revolutionary scheme.

The revolutionizing movement resulted in a number of changes that would prove consequential for the ensuing Cultural Revolution: Mao's writings acquired the stature of a red bible with absolute authority; humanism was viewed as bourgeois by its very nature and therefore to be rejected; class background became the key component in each individual's identity; offspring of veteran revolutionaries, referred to as "cadres' children," were designated as the people especially responsible to carry out the cause of revolution. The theme song of a popular Chinese children's movie, "The Red Kids," begins with a question, "Are you ready?" By the spring of 1966 our generation was by and large ready.

The Ideal Was to Become a "Bolt"

MA: I was disappointed that I didn't get into the school of my first choice, the prestigious Beijing Normal University's Affiliated Secondary School for Girls. A careless error I made in the entrance examination killed my chance. It was so unfair that the admission was determined solely by the result of one exam. I cried for a week when I learned that I was only admitted to my third and also last choice, the No. 8 Girls' Secondary School.

YE: But that was still a pretty good school.

MA: That was true. The school was on the site where Lu Xun once taught. That made me feel better about attending this school. I liked to sit by the tomb of the March eighteenth martyrs[1] in a quiet corner of the campus. In a room nearby, the bloodstained shirt of one martyr was on permanent display. I could even feel Lu Xun's presence in his old office, now occupied by the principal. Whenever I passed by that room, I would walk lightly as though Lu Xun's spirit were still there.

I remember my first day of school well. The courtyards were filled with laughing young women. We freshmen were constantly stopped by upper class students holding signs for clubs or sports teams. They asked whether we'd like to play basketball, or join the dance club, or maybe learn calligraphy. They looked so high-spirited and self-assured. And soon enough, I was elected to the school's Young Pioneer brigade committee, in charge of publishing the school wallpapers.

YE: You always stood out. Even though I got into the school of your first choice, I remained in the background. I also remember my first day of school because of a conversation I had with another new student. She told me she was a Young Pioneer brigade leader in her elementary school. Later I found out that a large number of my classmates had held posts either at the brigade or the company level in their elementary schools. I was thinking to myself, "Wow, here everybody is somebody." Eventually I made a few good friends among my classmates, but my class never evolved into a real *ban jiti* (class collective) like in elementary school. And none of my new teachers were like Teacher Wu.

But I do remember Teacher Wang with deep gratitude. She was our English teacher. Back then I didn't pay much attention to English because it was not a major academic subject. I only realized many years later when I began to resume English study on my own how solid a foundation Teacher Wang had laid for us. Teacher Wang was tall, slightly hunchbacked, and always soft-spoken. We respected her gentle manners and lucid lecturing style. She was a graduate of an American missionary school before 1949, which probably explained why her English was so good. But after class, she had little contact with us. Remembering my elementary school teachers, I was puzzled by her aloofness. Later I wondered whether she felt alienated by her students' increasingly radical political posture.

My experiences in the secondary school differed markedly from those in the elementary school. This had nothing to do with the different levels in the educational system per se. I think it had more to do with the major shift in the national political climate that began around that time.

MA: Wasn't it when the open rift with the Soviet Union occurred? I remember listening to the radio broadcasts of those editorials from *The People's Daily*,[2] the ones criticizing the Soviet Union as revisionist and a traitor to Marxism. Even though I didn't quite understand the content of the editorials, I was impressed by the forceful tone of the broadcasters' voices.

YE: The air smelt of gunpowder, so to speak, because of the militant tone of their voices. We were told that China was the last stronghold against both Soviet revisionism and U.S. imperialism. Supposedly both the Russians and the Americans were hoping China would change color through peaceful evolution. Dulles became a household name in China because of his notorious deathbed wish. Chairman Mao worried that we might not continue the revolutionary cause.

MA: Mao wrote something so captivating around this time that I can still recite by heart. It goes like this:

> The next few decades will be precious and important for the future of our country and the destiny of mankind. The twenty-year-old will be forty or fifty in twenty or thirty years' time. This generation of young people will take part in building our poor and bare country into a great strong socialist power and will fight and bury imperialism with their own hands. The task is arduous and the road long. Chinese people of lofty ambitions must dedicate their lives to the accomplishment of our great historic mission . . .[3]

Even today when I read this passage, tears come to my eyes . . . its patriotic passion still touches me.

YE: Somehow I see this passage in a different light. Several decades have indeed passed. But the world we find ourselves in now is totally different than the one Mao envisioned for us. It pains me to think how earnestly we once believed in the mission.

MA: At the time, statements like this really aroused my enthusiasm for revolution. I became aware of a special responsibility I had as a cadre's child (干部子女 / *ganbu zidi*). Until this point I was ignorant about family background and stuff like that. Right after I started secondary school, we were asked to fill out a personal information sheet in which there was a question about family background. I asked my father what to write and he said, "just write down *zhiyuan* (职员 / staff member)." He believed all government employees were staff members. But before long I began to realize that I was in a "red" category[4] as a revolutionary cadre's child. It made me feel real good. I had never thought that I was any different from my childhood friend Fan Lili. Now seeing myself in a new light, I started to hang around with girls from the same family background.

YE: Indeed. This family background business began to affect how we related to each other. My best friend in the class was a girl sitting next to me, and her family was not in the red category. We were able to remain friends until the Cultural Revolution began.

MA: Think about it, it is interesting that we all knew each other's family background.

YE: But it was not hard to find out. Around this time we were constantly asked to fill out personal information sheets. You only needed to look over another person's shoulder to see what she wrote down. We were all curious to know.

I guess family background had always been important in our society, but to define a person solely by it was new. Students from the so-called "five black categories"[5] began to be excluded from certain activities. My school was very close to the Chang'an Boulevard, the main avenue in Beijing. Whenever a foreign leader came for a state visit, classes were canceled and we would stand along the street to welcome the foreign delegation's motorcade. During one such event, the motorcade was nowhere in sight so I went back to the classroom to fetch something. I was surprised to see a classmate sitting by herself in the empty room. It suddenly occurred to me that she was there because her family was black so she was not allowed to welcome the foreign guests. We looked each other in the eye. She was composed. I felt awkward and didn't know what to say. It must be awful to be left alone.[6]

Another image of a student from a black family has also stuck with me. She was from a senior high class in my school. Once my class was working alongside her class during a rice harvest in a rural village. She outdid everyone in rice cutting and was also able to carry more bundles of rice than anybody else. Placing the bundles under her arms, she embraced them tightly by holding onto the edges of her sweat-soaked shirt. Completely focusing on what she was doing, she didn't seem to realize that other people could see her bare midriff. I watched her with amazement. Later we learned that she came from a black family. I wondered if she would be praised for her outstanding performance. I doubted she would because people from black families were supposed to make greater efforts to prove themselves. I felt sorry for her.

On the other hand, not everybody in the red categories was treated equally. Those from revolutionary cadre and revolutionary military families were more favored than those from worker and poor- and lower-middle peasant backgrounds. Once my school even held a meeting only for people in the first two categories. The meeting took place in the school's auditorium. Whenever we had meetings there, we had to bring our own chairs because there weren't enough seats in the auditorium. Dragging chairs caused much noise and the classroom looked empty afterwards. That day only about a dozen students left for the meeting, while the rest of the class silently remained in their seats. I felt uneasy and tried not to make too much noise.

The theme of the meeting was the special responsibility we had as offspring of veteran revolutionaries. The speaker, Hu Zhitao, was the deputy principal of our school. She gave an exuberant speech in which she said that our parents had contributed to the founding of the new nation and now it was our turn to play a big role in the revolutionary cause. Such a meeting fostered both a sense of responsibility and a sense of superiority.

MA: Although my school didn't hold meetings especially for cadres' children, I was very much taken with the idea of our special responsibility for the revolution. The message I received was not that we were superior to others, but that we shouldered a heavier burden.

YE: For me the most unforgettable event in this period is the revolutionizing movement. It was different from anything I'd experienced before. Suddenly there were meetings most afternoons in the time slots that used to be reserved for athletic and other extracurricular activities. Loudspeakers in every classroom bombarded us with news of the movement.

MA: We also had the revolutionizing movement in my school. Sometimes we had such long meetings that we ended up spending the night at school, sleeping on desks. I remember the two goals of the movement: to guard against Dulles' peaceful evolution and to continue the proletarian revolution.

YE: Were you also asked to "expose thoughts"? This aspect of the movement has left the deepest impression on me. The idea was that the more you dig up bad thoughts inside you, the more revolutionary you will become. What was a bad thought? Any "selfish" idea would do. If you envied somebody in your class, that was no good. If you looked down upon somebody in your class, that also was a bad thought.

MA: A girl in my grade confessed that when she ran a race, she often wished that the person in front of her would slip and fall. Another girl, after confessing her bad thoughts, felt so terrible about herself that she stood in the corridor the whole night, refusing to go inside.

YE: What kind of bad thought?

MA: I don't remember. All I know was that her classmates were scared that she might commit suicide, so they all stayed up with her. That girl was barely 14, yet she was totally wrapped up in blaming herself.

YE: A girl in my class confessed that she enjoyed strangers' attention on the street because of her good looks. Now she realized feeling good about such attention was bourgeois and unhealthy. What she said amused me because she really was not that good looking. But I also was amazed that she would share such private thoughts with us.

MA: But the point was that you were not supposed to hide *any* unhealthy thoughts from others.

YE: I found it hard to share my private thoughts. As a teenager I became interested in men. I noticed a delicate-looking young man whom I often saw reading at the Xinhua library. I was attracted by the melancholy expression on his face even though it was so out of tune with the increasingly revolutionized political climate. My taste would certainly be regarded as unhealthy, so I didn't say anything about it.

In my school the most commonly criticized bad thought was the desire to achieve fame, the kind of aspiration we used to feel proud to share, such as becoming an accomplished scientist or a well-known artist. A girl in my class criticized herself for dreaming about being an actress, surrounded by flowers after a successful performance. Such longing was now regarded as a bourgeois ambition. The new idea was to forget about personal glory. We were supposed to devote ourselves entirely to the revolution, do whatever the party asked us to do and be "bolts" that could be inserted anywhere.

As part of the revolutionizing scheme, we were sent to the countryside to help with the harvest. The idea was that strenuous physical labor could purify our thinking. Previously, if students in my school had done any physical labor, it was to pick strawberries on a farm in the suburbs. It sounded like a field trip to us. What we did was real agricultural work.

My first trip to a rural commune outside Beijing was in 1964, and it lasted for two weeks. As our truck approached the village, I saw something moving in front of us. It was a huge bundle of firewood. When we passed it, I realized it was a child of no more than ten years of age who was carrying a bundle four or five times his size. I was astonished. This was my first impression of rural China.

We were there to help with the rice harvest. Bending over one's body to cut rice with a sickle was backbreaking labor. But that was precisely the point. Some of my classmates saw this as a good opportunity to temper themselves. They worked zealously in the field and seldom stretched their bodies. I always fell behind. Even so, I got blisters all over my palms.

MA: We competed with each other to show that we were not afraid of "eating bitterness." What I remember most vividly was a long walk we took after a wheat harvest. The distance was 100 *li* (more than 30 miles). Don't forget it was after two weeks of intense physical labor. We started at dusk and didn't reach our destination until daybreak. My feet ached badly but I gritted my teeth and didn't say a word. In the middle of the night we were caught in a pouring rain and were soaked like drenched chickens, but nobody complained.

As soon as I returned home, I collapsed into my parents' soft bed. I slept for a whole day until dinnertime. When I got up, I walked with great difficulty like a crippled person. It was partly a show so that my mother would fuss over me and cook my favorite handmade noodles.

Next day I went back to school in the same sweat-soaked dirty pants and jacket I wore in the village. I wouldn't change into clean clothes and thought if I had done so it would mean that in my heart I detested rural life. When my mother asked me, "Why don't you take a bath and change into clean clothes?" I replied, "If I were still in the countryside, would I change clothes?" But to my surprise, I found all my classmates in clean clothes. I thought to myself, "Perhaps I should have changed mine as well."

YE: Before our first trip to the countryside, the school leaders held a briefing with us. What surprised me the most was their admonition to avoid contact with the local peasants. They said that the class situation in rural area was complicated, so don't greet anybody you meet and address a strange villager as "uncle" or "aunt." You could be talking to a former landlord or rich peasant. In the past we had always been taught to be polite to people. Now there was no need for courtesy. Rudeness was permitted.

About this time "Four clean-ups" Campaign was unfolding across the country. The main target was "unclean" cadres and "unreformed" former landlords and rich peasants. Class enemies were presumed to be everywhere, and we were told to be vigilant at all times.

MA: I remember a popular local opera where a former landlord's wife was trying to corrupt the party secretary with a bowl of sweet rice dumplings. She sang a long melody about how delicious the sweet tasted. Thinking about it now, how could a person be corrupted by a bowl of dumplings?

YE: The point was that class struggle was embedded in everyday life. In the village we didn't mingle with the local people. One evening while several of us were walking back to our dorm after supper, we saw some men squatting by the roadside. In the dark we could barely make out their faces. Motioning in their direction, a classmate whispered, "There could be a landlord there." We were all scared.

Many years later when I was a sent-down youth in Shanxi, I noticed that squatting was very common among peasant men. After dinner they liked to squat, smoking a pipe and chatting with neighbors. I then realized how ignorant we had been about peasant customs in our obsession with class struggle.

MA: I remember a discussion we had about this time in our political education class. A classmate raised a question, "If you see a man drowning but don't know his class status, would you throw yourself into the water to save his life? What if the person turns out to be a former landlord? Is it worth risking your life?" We had endless debate. Some argued that there would be no time to find out a dying person's class identity. One should simply jump into the water and save a life. Others asked what if he *was* a former landlord? A good life might be sacrificed to save a bad life. Even the teacher didn't know what to say.

YE: This debate was so revealing of the time. In the past we had been taught that when somebody's life was in danger, we should try to save it, period. A life was a life. But now the first question we were supposed to ask was the person's class status. If the person didn't belong to the right class, his or her life might not be worth saving. No wonder your classmates were confused. One may say that failure to help "a class enemy" in trouble presaged the upcoming violent behavior toward class enemies once the Cultural Revolution began.

In my school some students started to publicly criticize their own parents. One day I heard a speech by a senior high student. The girl's parents were well-known public figures, her father, a nonparty high ranking official, was also a prominent scholar, and her mother was an accomplished calligrapher. From the loudspeaker their daughter told the entire school that she often thought her mother was rather coarse, and that she felt ashamed of her. I couldn't believe my ears. How could she talk about her parent like this in public? Did her mother know? Of course at this point I had no idea that exposing one's parents would become a politically fashionable thing to do during the Cultural Revolution.

MA: It seems that you were harboring some misgivings about the movement.

YE: I felt more and more out of tune with the time. This was when Chairman Mao's works were elevated to the status of a red bible. Some people claimed that they had been transformed by a particular article or even just a few lines by Mao, but I was skeptical. One day my class was repairing the school sports ground. We worked in pairs; two people carried a basket of dirt on a pole. A classmate and I worked together. We had made several trips and the basket on our shoulders felt heavier and heavier. Suddenly this girl paused, turned to me and declared, "I'm just thinking of a quotation from Chairman Mao and the basket feels much lighter." My mental response was, "Really?" Of course I didn't utter it.

MA: I think your classmate was telling you her true feeling at the moment.

YE: She probably was. But I was just a little unconvinced of the magical power of Chairman Mao's words.

MA: I would absolutely not have questioned what your classmate said. Stories filled the newspapers now about how people were able to create miracles once armed with Chairman Mao's thoughts.

YE: I couldn't make myself believe everything in the paper, but of course I was not immune to the powerful political rhetoric around us. It was a stressful period for me. I knew some of my thoughts were improper, perhaps even dangerous. As a cadre's child, I was supposed to be even more revolutionary than others. I felt guilty that I did not live up to that high standard. At meetings I made self-criticisms for not being a good revolutionary. But I found it impossible to persuade myself that my own thinking and feelings were all wrong. I was torn by an acute inner pain, something I had never experienced before. Both my parents sensed that I didn't quite fit with the times. My mother called me *mingshipai* (名士派 / a lofty scholar), her nickname for me around this time. My father was more seriously concerned and had long conversations with me a couple of times, but he didn't try to force me to change.

My moodiness didn't escape people at school either. In a conversation with me, a teacher observed that I looked too low-spirited for a youth living in the Mao era. I thought to myself, "Somebody has noticed." Then came a moment when I realized that I was being excluded from the revolutionary circle.

You know nothing was more important for people of our age group than to join the Communist Youth League.[7] It was like an admission into the "big revolutionary family." In my class most cadres' children almost automatically joined the youth organization once they reached the age of 15. When did you join?

MA: On my fifteenth birthday. But there wasn't such a rule in my school to automatically admit cadres' children. That would be regarded as a special treatment.

YE: There wasn't such a rule in my school either, but it was the reality in my class. By the spring of 1966 almost every cadre's child had been admitted into the league except me and another girl. The day when I saw on the blackboard the announcement of the league membership for the youngest student in my class, who was also a cadre's child, a friend noticed that I blushed. I felt excluded. To put it lightly, it was like a bunch of kids not including me in their game. But in that fervent revolutionary atmosphere, joining the league was like joining the revolution, and it was a serious matter. The pressure on those who were still outside the league was high, especially for someone like me. I knew how to get into the league. It was just a matter of a few thought reports. But I didn't want to write them.

MA: But if you didn't let the league get to know your thinking, how could they take you in?

YE: In my class one girl was very eager to join the league. Once she deliberately left her diary open on her desk so that other people could read it. Her diary contained nothing but her reflections on Chairman Mao's works. I was turned off by this calculated act. She was not from a red family. A cadre's child didn't need to try this hard. A few thought reports would do, but I thought they were phony.

MA: I still don't understand why you could be detached when everybody else was so absorbed with the revolutionary fever.

YE: I have thought about this question myself. I think it had something to do with my upbringing. My parents always let us express our opinions and that allowed me to develop independent thinking. During this intensely revolutionary period, although my father was worried about me politically, my parents continued to respect me as an individual and largely left me alone. I didn't know until much later how worried my father actually was.

The fact that I had politically questionable relatives on both sides of my family had some effect on my political identity. I always felt uneasy filling out personal information sheets because of a specific question: "Do you have relatives that have been executed or imprisoned?" My fifth uncle was in prison and I had to say "yes" to the question. Unlike some cadres' children who liked to boast about the redness of their families, I knew mine was not without stains. This awareness cast a shadow over me and humbled me somewhat.

My liberal tendency also had something to do with the culture of the Xinhua compound. I guess different compounds generated different atmosphere. As the national news agency, Xinhua was probably more liberal than a military compound or a compound that housed, say the Ministry of Mining. It might even have a slight cosmopolitan flavor. The people working at Xinhua were more exposed to what was going on both in China and in the world. After an important international conference, for instance, the head of Xinhua would give employees a briefing. Well-known national figures would often be invited to speak. The gate of the auditorium was usually not guarded, so I could sneak in and sit in the back of the balcony.

Sometimes I even glimpsed a world that I was not supposed to see. Xinhua once had a photo exhibition to show how the Soviet Union had deteriorated into a revisionist country. In one photo several Russian girls were leaning against a stage, looking up at a young American pianist who had just finished a performance. The eyes of the girls were shining and flowers were scattered all over. I guess this photo was meant to demonstrate how decadent Western culture was corrupting people in the Soviet Union. But to me, the young man and women together with the piano and the flowers made an enchanting scene.

"I Wanted to Look Like a Soldier"

MA: Unlike you, I was totally drawn into the revolutionary high tide. The greatest impact of the revolutionizing movement was on my appearance. I was convinced that being a revolutionary meant a complete break from a bourgeois life style, so I went to extremes to look simple and plain, because that was the image of a committed revolutionary. In those days you could still find nicely dressed women walking in the street with permed hair and high-heeled shoes. I despised them.

YE: But you used to adore beautiful things.

MA: I was that way as a little girl. Once I saw a foreign movie about a fairy tale and was thrilled by the crown and cloak worn by the princess. Afterward I made a paper crown and used a bath-towel as a substitute for the cloak. Putting them on, I looked at myself in the mirror and felt great. I often drew beautiful women clad in traditional Chinese costumes. My father thought my drawings were really good. As a girl I wore my hair in braids. My mother liked to experiment with my hair in various ways, sometimes making me look like a maiden in ancient China.

When the revolutionizing movement began, I had my hair cut short— short hair looked more revolutionary. Every time my mother cut my hair I would insist "shorter, still shorter!" This would drive my mother crazy. "How can it be any shorter? Your hair hardly covers your ears!" My hair would look fluffy after the haircut. I would shampoo it and go to bed right away so that I could flatten the hair down. Otherwise I would look really stupid.

Up to this point we girls followed certain fashion trends, such as dressing one's hair in certain ways or showing a beautiful collar outside jacket. But now all that was gone. I stopped wearing brightly colored outfits and would prefer old clothes with patches. Having patches on one's clothes became the latest fashion.

YE: Like you, I also shed nice-looking dresses and skirts to put on pants and loosely cut jackets. If you think about it, didn't our mothers always wear plain clothes? My mother dressed like a typical woman cadre always in simple out-fits. But she did have some nice clothing. I remember a Chinese style silk jacket in a bright blue color. But when she wore it, she always put a plain outer garment over it, so you could hardly see the fine fabric inside.

MA: You remind me of a cream-colored Western woolen skirt my mother had. Once, I think it was toward the end of the Cultural Revolution, my mother took it out from the bottom of a chest and said to me, "Here, you can have it." I was surprised, "Is this yours?" I never saw my mother wear it. It seemed too fancy for her.

YE: A year or so before my mother's death, I went with her to a neighbor-hood department store. In front of a fabric counter she suddenly said, "If I were young, I would wear (nice clothes)." She was at a late stage of Alzheimer's, yet she was able to express such a clear wish. Whenever I think about my mother's remarks, I feel sad.

Throughout most of my mother's life she was always in plain and simple clothes. Her influence on me in this area was silent but must be very power-ful. I went along with the revolutionary fashion trend without any resent-ment, even though I was somewhat detached from the overall revolutionizing scheme. In elementary school I had a fascination with high-heeled shoes. I could draw a fashionable-looking shoe with just one stroke. No more such drawings now. I would definitely be criticized if I had continued to do so.

Recently I came across two old photos that showed how drastic the change in our appearance was at the time. One was a class picture of my elementary school, taken in the summer of 1963. We girls were all wearing brightly colored skirts and the boys were in shorts. The other was a photo of my middle school class, taken around 1965. Almost all the girls were clad in grey and dark blue clothes. The colors were gone. I would not have realized that the transformation was so drastic without the reminder of these photos. What's amazing is that the whole process seemed so natural. I didn't feel that I was being deprived of anything.

MA: It didn't cause me any agony either. As a matter of fact, I wholeheart-edly embraced the new fashion ideal and ardently pursued it. I *wanted* to look plain and simple. To be precise, I wanted to look like a soldier. Part of the reason I had my hair cut so short was to imitate a character in the film, "Youth in the Battle Fire." I was a great admirer of Gao Shan, a character in the film. I adored her for her ability to disguise herself as a man among male soldiers. There was another film I also liked very much, "The Red Detachment of Women." After seeing it I yearned to wear army uniforms like the slave girls-turned-soldiers. I envied these women warriors. Why did they get to fight like men and I didn't?

Around this time a Mao's poem praising women militia was frequently cited. It went something like "Chinese daughters have high aspiring minds / they love their battle array, not silk and satins."[8] The image of the daring women militia stuck in my mind.

With these women as models, I tried hard to avoid things that would interest "ordinary" women. For instance, I knew nothing about cooking. When I heard people say, "The meat is too *lao* (meaning overcooked)." I would ask, "What is *lao*?" When the name of a fabric was mentioned, I would ask what it was. People thought I lacked basic knowledge about everyday life. But this was precisely what I wanted. Why should I bother myself with the trivial stuff? I was also turned off by the way women were depicted in some books. They described women's laughter as "giggling." Why couldn't women have hearty "ha ha" laughter?

YE: Ha ha, that was true . . . and it still is.

MA: I was convinced that women "giggle" in order to please men. I also resented talks such as "don't feel so good because we girls are academically ahead of boys now. Wait till we go to senior high school and college. Boys will catch up and surpass us." I couldn't bear the message that ultimately we were not as intelligent as men.

I had one final resentment. My big elder brother worked in an agricultural technology school in the suburbs of Beijing. I sometimes went to visit him there. One day I heard someone say, "As soon as a woman gets married and has children, she's finished." I hated this. I said to myself that I would never fall into that trap. I would succeed even if all other women failed.

Those days I wanted to be just like men. There were numerous male heroes in books and movies for us to emulate. My favorites were Paul and Gadfly.[9] Thinking about it now, it is interesting that both of them were foreigners: one was a red army soldier in the Russian revolution and the other a freedom fighter in the Italian nationalist liberation movement. What impressed me the most about Gadfly was his ability to endure sufferings. He once said, "A real man is somebody who is able to endure hardships and never complains." This was the quality of a true revolutionary.

Paul and Gadfly, along with Gao Shan and the soldiers in the Red Detachment of Women were all people who lived in exciting war times. I loved books and films on war. I often thought that it was a shame I was not born in wartime. I missed the opportunity to become a hero.

YE: You thought so? I didn't have the urge to become a hero. I also knew these stories, but they didn't have as much an impact on me. I found characters such as the son in Turgenev's *Father and Son* interesting. He was an ambivalent character, full of contradictions, not a hero type.

Speaking of revolutionary heroes, I found Lu Jiachuan, a character in the novel *The Song of Youth* (青春之歌 / *qingchun zhi ge*) quite charming. I liked his casual demeanor. He was a devoted revolutionary but he didn't act in a self-righteous way, and he didn't take himself too seriously.

If you think about it, our education was filled with contradictions. On the one hand we were told to be bolts and obedient tools of the party and the nation. On the other hand there was so much talk about revolutionary heroism. If you strived very hard for something but in the end were not recognized, wouldn't you feel let down?

MA: I didn't think about fame and recognition. I just longed to live a thrilling life like the heroes in books and on screen. What I couldn't bear was being mundane.

YE: You were able to find books and movies that inspired you, but many things I liked would end up being criticized. For a while I was fascinated by detective stories. My favorite was *The Moonstone* by the English writer Wilkie Collins. One day I brought the book to school and a classmate noticed a Victorian lady in one illustration. She told me right away that this book was "unhealthy" and I shouldn't read it. I found that much of what I had read in the past, such as Chinese folklore, Western fairy tales, and classical literature were now being criticized as non-proletarian, feudalist, or bourgeois. No more Snow White or little mermaid. I was expected to reject the literature and ideals I had learned to treasure in my childhood. I found this most difficult to do.

MA: Among the movies under attack at this time, there were some I also liked . . . at least initially, such as "Early Spring" (早春二月 / *zaochun eryu*) and "Sisters on Stage" (舞台姐妹 / *wutai jiemei*). The former concerned a young intellectual in the 1920s who, out of sympathy for a young widow whose husband was killed in a battle, decided to marry her rather than the woman he truly loved. The film was criticized for its bourgeois humanism. I didn't understand why it was wrong for the man to help a poor woman, but I persuaded myself that the criticism must be right and I should overcome my petty-bourgeois sentimentality. Whenever doubts came into my mind, I would tell myself that I should correct my own wrong thinking.

YE: You also mentioned "Sisters on Stage." One criticism about that movie was a line said by an old *yue* opera singer before his death: "live your life in integrity, pursue your art in earnest" (清清白白做人，任任真真唱戏 / *qingqing baibai zuoren, renren zhenzhen changxi*).[10] It was criticized because it was only concerned with maintaining individual integrity and was not about how to fight against the ugly old society in the mass revolution. But the line struck a chord in me. As I repeated it silently to myself, I thought, "It is so well-said."

MA: Really? I definitely would have rejected that line. It didn't sound revolutionary to me.

YE: But I liked it. What's wrong with guarding one's integrity and being diligent in one's pursuit?

Your role models were either determined woman warriors or high-minded male revolutionaries. What about love? Did it have a place in the revolution?

MA: Yes. I was deeply moved by the love between Gadfly and Gemma. The two had lost contact for many years. When they met again, Gemma did not recognize Gadfly because his face had changed so much. For his part, Gadfly avoided Gemma because he thought he was going to die. At the end of the novel when he was about to be executed, Gadfly wrote a letter to Gemma in which he said, "I will forever remain a big happy gadfly." This line touched my heart.

YE: It seemed that for us love was a beautiful spiritual thing worth pursuing, but it had nothing to do with either sex or everyday life. I remember reading a scene in *The Song of Youth*. After the death of her lover Lu Jiachuan, Lin Daojing threw herself into revolutionary work to divert herself from pain. She was working under a new leader, Jiang Hua. The two got along well but nothing was personal. One day Jiang Hua expressed his feelings toward Lin. When it was getting late at night, he said to her, "I'm not leaving tonight." Lin was silent for a while and then replied, "Fine." And that was it.

MA: So they had sex?

YE: Apparently, but it was only vaguely implied. When I first read the novel I didn't understand what was going on. Why did this guy want to stay? Now when I think about the dialogue between the two, I laugh at my naïveté.

MA: Talking about ignorance on sexuality, I had no knowledge about my body and was caught completely unprepared when I first had my period. Nobody had ever warned me about it, not even my mother. Then she told me it would happen to me every month. This was the first time I'd learned that a big physiological difference existed between men and women. I was so shocked. I had always thought that women could simply put on men's clothes, like the soldiers in the "Red Detachment," and we would be like men.

YE: My mother didn't say anything to me about menstruation either. But before I began menstruating, I was already aware that something mysterious was going on among some girls in my class. When they had "it" they would be excused from physical education class, which puzzled and upset the boys. I envied their privilege and didn't view menstruation as terrifying.

But I had an imaginary fear about rape when I was 13 or 14. Maybe it was an indication that some physical change was taking place in my body, since we lived in a society where actual rape cases were rarely heard. For a while I was gripped by the fear and obsessed with this question: if I were raped, should I continue to live or should I commit suicide? I couldn't answer the question. I was tormented.

MA: Did you talk to anyone about your fear?

YE: No, I kept it to myself. As I think about it now, I realize how powerful the age-old notion of chastity was, that is, the idea that women were supposed to be pure and chaste. If physically violated, better kill yourself.

MA: But women of our generation didn't hear that kind of talk. It belonged to the old society.

YE: Chastity was still a highly desirable quality for women. In novels and movies made in the 1950s and 1960s, bad women were often sexually "loose."

MA: That's true. . . . When I was 13 or 14, I started having thoughts about men and women, even though I knew nothing about sex. One day, it suddenly occurred to me that Chairman Mao must have had relationships with women. Otherwise how could he have had children? I felt extremely guilty about this thought, as though I had committed a big crime. The guilt feeling stayed with me for about six months, like a dark heavy shadow hanging over me. I'm still puzzled by why in the world it was Mao who turned up in my sexual fantasies. Maybe it was because he was like a superman to us—he was everywhere.

YE: My sexual fantasy expressed itself in a different way. Also at around this age, I began to sketch "unhealthy" pictures. When the Cultural Revolution began, people from my father's department searched our home and took my drawings away.

MA: I can guess what you drew. They must have been naked human bodies.

YE: Yes, they were nude female bodies. I had a diary book given to me by my mother as a present. Inside were many beautiful prints. The ones that most fascinated me were Xu Beihong's[11] nude sketches. I didn't feel guilty about these drawings, but I definitely wanted to keep them my secret.

MA: For a while I was also drawing female bodies. I wanted to draw them nude but in the end I always put clothes on. One day I finally drew a nude body. When I realized what I had done, I blushed and quickly erased it. Afterward I experienced another period of intense guilt.

* * *

Without knowing it, we were approaching the Cultural Revolution. In the spring of 1966, the residents of Xinhua compound learned that PLA soldiers would replace Xinhua's own security staff to guard the work area. What the news meant for us children was the loss of access to the library and other facilities in the work area. I was very upset and wrote a "big character poster" protesting the restriction. I argued that in order to become revolutionary successors, we needed to have access to good books and journals, and therefore the library should continue to be open to us.

My poster attracted attention of the people at the department in charge of political education at Xinhua, who particularly disliked the tone in the poster. I had written in a style that was casual and somewhat sarcastic as I was tired of writings in the newspapers that read like sermons. Those people thought children of the Mao era shouldn't write this way. It showed that my thinking was "complicated."

My father was not in Beijing so they talked to my mother and asked her to pay attention to my thinking. I was not a Xinhua employee and only a teenager, yet they thought my thinking was their business. My mother told me briefly what they had said, but she didn't make a big deal of it. My concern was about the access to the library. What I didn't realize was the tighter security precaution at a politically sensitive organization like the Xinhua News Agency foreboded that a severe political storm was gathering.

"Take Up Pens as Guns"

At the height of the Cultural Revolution in the summer of 1966 a song was heard across the country:

> *Take up pens as guns,*
> *Concentrate fire on the reactionary gang!*
> *Whoever dares to say a bad word about the Party,*
> *Send him to the Kingdom of Hell at once!*

This was the song of the Red Guards, a youth organization originally founded in Beijing in late May of 1966 by a group of secondary school students. Mostly cadres' children, they saw themselves as "the red guards of Chairman Mao." On August 18 of the same year Mao brought the young rebels to national attention by receiving them from the balcony of Tiananmen (The Gate of Heavenly Peace), himself clad in full army uniform with a Red Guard band around his arm. Immediately following Mao's dramatic appearance at this critical juncture of the Cultural Revolution, the Red Guard movement swept the entire country.

For Ma Xiaodong and me, the first several months of the Cultural Revolution were most unforgettable. What happened can hardly be explained rationally. Apparently believing that much of China's state apparatus had been contaminated by bourgeois revisionism, Mao was determined to cleanse the party and the government he himself had helped found to ensure that China remained committed to revolutionary ideals. Eventually almost anyone in a responsible position was persecuted, be it president of the state, head of a government agency, or leader of a school. They were labeled variously as "power holders taking the capitalist road" (走资派), "black gangsters" (黑帮), or simply "ox ghosts and snake spirits" (牛鬼蛇神). Meanwhile, previous state enemies such as former landlords, rightists, and counter-revolutionaries were not spared by this new round of political persecution. Wall posters provided the means by which enemies were exposed, grievances of all kinds were voiced, and issues were raised and debated. Public struggle meetings were the most common form of condemnation and humiliation, where targeted individuals were separated from their accusers and denounced. These meetings were often accompanied with violence.

Secondary schools in Beijing were among the first to feel the heat of the Cultural Revolution. Teenage students, baptized in the revolutionizing campaigns taking place on their campuses prior to the Cultural Revolution, were eager to respond to Mao's call. The most radical tended to be those from cadres' background, as they had prided themselves on being the true heirs of the revolution. Both Ma Xiaodong and I found ourselves caught in the center of a political whirlpool. Our memories of this tumultuous time consist of a series of "moments." The most striking one for me was when I learned the brutal death of my school's party secretary as a result of student beating. For Ma Xiaodong, it was seeing her mother's hair shaved in the humiliating "yin / yang" fashion after a fierce struggle meeting at her school. Both incidents occurred in August, the month of "red terror."

I was more willing to share my experiences and observations, while Ma Xiaodong held back a bit initially. Only later did she finally come forth, surprising me with her very moving recollections. Obviously the wounds still hurt.

Chronology of major events mentioned in our conversation:

November 1965   *Publication of Yao Wenyuan's article "The Dismissal of Hai Rui from Office" in a Shanghai newspaper. Yao's article is usually viewed as the first signal for the upcoming Cultural Revolution.*

May 1966   *The fall of Peng Zhen, mayor of Beijing and a member of the CCP politburo. Peng and three other top party and government officials were accused of forming an "anti-party" clique. When the news became public, it had the effect of a political earthquake, albeit a mild one in light of what was to come later.*

The exposure of Deng Tuo, along with two other leading officials in the Beijing municipal government as members of the anti-party "Three-Family Village." Deng Tuo was a talented writer and learned scholar. Some of his essays were being criticized as satires on the Great Leap Forward.

Toward the end of the month some students at the Affiliated Secondary School to Qinghua University founded a student organization called "Red Guards."

June 1, 1966   *Publication of the editorial "Sweeping away the Ox Ghosts and Snake Spirits" in the People's Daily. It pronounced that "the high tide of a stormy proletarian Cultural Revolution has risen in our country." Subsequently students at secondary schools and colleges in Beijing stopped academic studies to throw themselves wholeheartedly to making the revolution.*

July 18, 1966   *Mao returned to Beijing from his prolonged stay in the south. Soon afterward he instructed the withdrawal of work teams that had been dispatched in the month of June to many schools after the school authorities collapsed. The idea of sending work teams, which Mao had earlier approved, was now criticized as "reactionary." Work teams began to leave schools at the end of the month.*

Around the time when work teams were leaving, a couplet appeared across many secondary schools in Beijing. It went like: "If the father's a hero, the son's a great fellow. If the father's a reactionary, the son's a rotten egg." Heated debates about the couplet were held everywhere. The appearance of the couplet further divided the student body into two basic camps: those from "red" families, primarily children of revolutionary cadres and military men, and those not. It greatly heightened an already much inflated sense of superiority among the "red children."

August 1, 1966   *Mao wrote a letter to support the Red Guards at the Affiliated Secondary School to Qinghua University, in which he praised the youngsters for their "revolutionary rebellious spirit."*

August 1–12, 1966   *The eleventh plenum of the eighth CCP's convention was held in Beijing. Liu Shaoqi was demoted and his Cultural Revolution policies were criticized. Lin Bao was promoted to the No.2 position in the party.*

August 18, 1966   *Mao received Red Guards, mostly students from Beijing, on the balcony of Tiananmen. Anti Four-Olds Campaign soon swept the the country. Mao would receive Red Guards from all over the country eight more times in the following months until the end of November.*

September 1966   *Beginning of the great linkup. It lasted for several months and eventually ended as the winter season approached.*

October 3, 1966   *Publication of the editorial, "March on the Road of Chairman Mao's Thought" in the thirteenth issue of the Red Flag, the official journal of the CCP. It made clear that the main target of the Cultural Revolution was "reactionary bourgeois line" represented by Liu Shaoqi and Deng Xiaoping. The Cultural Revolution Small Group turned to support a new group of rebels, abandoning the original Red Guards, whose parents now were the targets of the revolution. The couplet about "heroes" and "rotten eggs" was now criticized as representing a "bloodline" theory.*

December 1966   *The emergence of "The Capital Red Guards United Action Committee" (shoudu hongweibing lianhe xingdong weiyuan hui or simply liandong). This was a loosely knit organization that appealed to the original Red Guards. It openly defied the authority of the Cultural Revolution Small Group led by Mao's wife Jiang Qing and explicitly challenged the premises of the Cultural Revolution. It had an inherited flaw: it was too much entangled with the bloodline thinking.*

During this time more and more people managed to get out of the political whirlpool, turning themselves into "bystanders."

"I'm Liberated!"

YE: I associated the summer of 1966 with hibiscus flowers, in blossom on a row of trees I passed on my way to school. Their delicate texture and soft pink color contrasted so sharply with the iron and blood character of that summer. Maybe this was why the flowers have resonated with me.

Tension crackled in the air ever since Yao Wenyuan's article appeared. That spring term, my last in junior high, we were supposed to prepare for the senior high entrance exam. But my classmates and I could hardly concentrate on academic studies. Somehow we sensed the seriousness of the situation. Language in the papers became increasingly hyper and militant. Every day new targets were exposed and new charges were made. After class we discussed what we read in the newspapers and exchanged news and rumors. Even so, the final outbreak of the Cultural Revolution seemed sudden to me.

MA: For me, *The People's Daily* editorial "Sweeping Away the Ox Ghosts and Snake Spirits" signaled the beginning of the Cultural Revolution. From that day on all we did was make revolution. No more classes.

YE: It was a memorable day for me too. Everything appeared normal that morning. At the swimming class we had later in the morning I was chatting with a friend about the bad fortune of one classmate. We heard that her father, the head of the National Drama Association, had just been exposed. It didn't occur to us that the same fate would soon befall our own families. Neither did we truly understand what "being exposed" meant. We had a good time playing in the water.

When we returned to school from the public swimming pool, the whole campus was covered with wall posters, denouncing school leaders for carrying out a revisionist educational line. Most of the posters were written by senior high students. We had left for no more than three hours for the swimming class and yet our world was forever changed. I found out later that on the same day wall posters appeared in secondary schools across Beijing. Even till this day I am amazed by how prepared some students were. For one thing, where did they get all the paper, brushes, and ink to write the posters in such a short time? It was as if they were all ready, just waiting for a command to act. *The People's Daily's* editorial signaled that command.

The swimming class was my last class before the Cultural Revolution. I had to wait for more than seven years to go back to a real classroom. Most of my classmates' education, however, was permanently terminated. On that day in early June, we were abruptly jolted from our familiar trajectory and harshly thrown into a bizarre new world. Nothing was certain any more. School leaders became *heibang* (black gangsters), and parents were under attack.

MA: I felt more excited than you at the beginning of the Cultural Revolution. I was happy that there were no more classes. I kept saying to myself, "I'm liberated!" Although I had been a good student, I never liked the monotony of the classroom. When I heard Chairman Mao's criticism of the educational system,[12] I felt he was speaking directly to me. I wholeheartedly agreed that students should become masters of their own academic studies and be free from the pressure of grades.

YE: But Mao had made the criticism a year ago; it wasn't new at the beginning of the Cultural Revolution.

MA: Yet nothing had really changed. For me it was a big relief that the old order finally collapsed. I still strongly believe that the educational system we had prior to the Cultural Revolution was seriously flawed. I particularly resented the entrance examination system—one single test determined a person's fate. It had happened to me.

YE: I didn't harbor the same resentment as you against the educational system. With the interruption of classes, we naturally stopped preparing for the senior high entrance exam. I don't remember having any particular reaction to it. I vaguely sensed that what was going on was larger than educational reform.

MA: My enthusiasm at the beginning of the Cultural Revolution also reflected my yearning for more thrills in life. I had always wished to be born during the time of war. Now my turn had finally come. My spirits were very high. I was busy making revolution and often didn't go home for days. At night we put a few desks together as beds and slept in the classroom. I was so excited that I didn't need much sleep.

YE: I shared some of your excitement. I was captivated by the full name of the Cultural Revolution: the Historically Unprecedented Great Proletarian Cultural Revolution. It sounded galvanizing. I felt I was participating in the making of history. It was a grand feeling. I was in this mood when we marched in a parade hailing the launch of the Cultural Revolution after the publication of *The People's Daily*'s editorial. We just walked around the school campus, shouting slogans and so forth. The parade was led by school leaders, even though the campus was now covered with posters denouncing them. As soon as the parade was over I heard some students say that when the deputy principal, Hu Zhitao, was shouting slogans, she only raised her right arm. It meant that she supported rightists in her heart. This was absurd.

MA: You already saw the absurdity?

YE: Just in this particular case. I thought the charge was ridiculous. Wasn't it natural that we right-handed people raised our right arms when we shouted slogans?

It was clear that the school leaders had lost respect. The students were pretty happy about this, but some teachers were worried. They warned us privately not to oppose the school leadership. They said that the current situation resembled that of 1957 when people at first were encouraged to criticize the leaders, but later were purged for doing so. The lesson of 1957, it turned out, didn't apply to the Cultural Revolution. This time Mao was dismantling his own power base. It was indeed unprecedented.

MA: The leadership in my school also quickly collapsed. Soon afterward a work team[13] arrived to take over the leadership role. We learned later that it was Liu Shaoqi and Deng Xiaoping[14] who had decided to send the work teams. Mao was not even in Beijing at this time.

After the arrival of the work team, much of the initial excitement diminished. The work team tried to bring order to school. Every day we spent most of the time sitting in the classroom studying Chairman Mao's works and editorials in *The People's Daily*. It was boring. Occasionally there would be a meeting or two to criticize school leaders. The speakers were appointed by the work team. My enthusiasm was fading.

It seemed to me that the regrouping of students was the most important thing happening right then. My class was immediately divided into two camps: cadres' children and non-cadres' children. I, of course, only hung around with people from red families.

YE: I also found myself in a new position. Membership in the Youth League no longer mattered. The only thing that counted was family background. I naturally belonged to the group of cadres' children. My best friend was not from a cadre's family, and now we found each other in separate camps. Whenever I saw her I felt uneasy. On the other hand, it wasn't a bad thing to be in a privileged position. Besides, nobody cared anymore that I wasn't a league member.

When the cadres' children were together, we didn't engage in anything particularly high-minded. What we often did, as a matter of fact, was gossip. We liked to give nicknames to other classmates, especially those pretty-looking ones. When I heard some funny names, I would have a good laugh, even though I knew it was rather disgusting. Before the Cultural Revolution we didn't treat our fellow students this way. Now in the name of revolution the ugly side of human nature shamelessly revealed itself.

Many posters in my school accused former school leaders of favoring students from black families while discriminating against cadres' children. This charge was totally groundless because cadres' children had already been elevated to a high position before the Cultural Revolution. On the other hand, there were indeed some students whom I felt didn't receive fair treatment. They were students recruited from rural areas outside Beijing, possibly as some sort of political gesture, and they were placed in one class. With their rural accent and "country bumpkin" looks, these students clearly did not fit into an elite urban school. When the Cultural Revolution began, nobody ever spoke on their behalf. Instead what I heard was a lot of baloney about alleged discrimination against cadres' children.

My feelings were mixed at this time. Part of me liked my new status, part of me felt uneasy, and a third part resented what was going on. The fact that high cadres' children dominated the scene in my school really turned me off. The work team set up Cultural Revolution committees in every class and grade. More often than not the head of a committee was the daughter of a high official. This was nepotism in its most naked form. Before the Cultural Revolution high cadres' children didn't draw that much attention. Now they were celebrities. It seemed that they formed an exclusive club that admitted only the reddest blood. If people like me stood above the students from non-cadres' families, then they were above us. It was hierarchy within hierarchy. This reality made me feel that the Cultural Revolution was their show, not mine. I wondered whether I would have had such a grudge if I had been in a school where there wasn't such a concentration of high cadres' children. I might have felt less ambivalent and enjoyed my newly elevated status more.

MA: I also felt somewhat uneasy about my new status. A couplet appeared around this time that pushed the obsession with bloodline to the extreme. It went something like this: "If the father's a hero, the son's a great fellow. If the father's a reactionary, the son's a rotten egg" (老子英雄儿好汉, 老子反动儿混蛋 / *laozi yingxiong er haohan; laozi fandong er hundan*).[15] I don't know who authored the couplet, but it sure stirred an uproar. My school held several heated debates about it. Those who opposed it argued that a person's political destiny shouldn't be determined by her birth. Individual performance should also count. This made sense to me, since I also thought that the couplet was too absolute. But in the end I went along with it. After all, I belonged to the "great fellows."

YE: If I remember correctly, the couplet appeared in my school after the withdrawal of the work team. Mao returned to Beijing in late July and accused work teams of "oppressing the revolutionary masses." After the work teams left, one might say all shackles were removed from us. The Cultural Revolution really began in earnest. The couplet happened to appear at this chaotic juncture. Alongside the couplet I saw a wall poster in my school saying that cadres' children differed from other kids from the day of birth.

The first word other babies uttered was "mom," whereas cadres' children learned to say "long live Chairman Mao" as soon as they could speak.

MA: Really? This was ridiculous.

YE: Indeed. How could anyone believe such nonsense? But I didn't have the moral courage to stand up and challenge the couplet—it was easier to go along with it than to oppose it. The couplet brought discrimination against people from black families to new heights. Now called "bastards' kids," they could be openly insulted in public places and were often refused service in a bus or a restaurant.

MA: The couplet was even made into a song called "The Song of Rebellion." It started with the couplet and followed with these lines: "Come and stand on our side if you want to be a revolutionary. Damn you and get lost if you don't!" I didn't like the song. It was too vulgar. Later it was also made into a dance and the movements were crude. My gymnastic background made it hard for me to swallow such coarse stuff.

YE: But coarseness was now in vogue. I actually learned to sing the song with a group of girls. Now that I think about it, it must have been a Red Guard activity. We paused before the line that contained the words "damn you" and "get lost." Many of us laughed out of embarrassment. Then we proceeded and uttered the crude words in one voice. Again we laughed. I think this time there was a triumphant note in our laughter as if we had overcome an obstacle. It was the first time I ever spoke in such language. I didn't realize it could be fun; it was almost liberating.

We also became more extreme in our appearance. Some girls in my school cut their hair very short. A few even shaved their heads. From the back you could hardly tell whether it was a girl or a boy. Some folded their pants to the knees and walked barefoot.

MA: Many girls in my school dropped their feminine-sounding names and adopted gender neutral and more revolutionary ones, such as "Weidong" (defending Mao Zedong) and "Dongbing" (the soldier of Mao Zedong).

YE: I changed my name too. I kept the sound "li" but changed the character from the one that means "beautiful" (丽) to the one that means "strength" (力). Beauty was useless. What I needed now was strength.

"Bian Zhongyun Is Dead—That Is It"

YE: What shocked me the most in the Cultural Revolution was the eruption of violence. It didn't happen right away. At first my class could still sit down and debate on what would be the proper way to treat those "problematic" individuals, whether it should be in a mild manner like *hefeng xiyu* (和风细雨 / breeze and light rain) or in a harsh way like *jifeng baoyu* (急风暴雨 / strong wind and thunderstorm). Mao mentioned both approaches in his works. Those days one had to quote Chairman Mao to bolster one's argument.

I was on the side that advocated breeze and light rain. We believed that a tender approach would be the most effective way to help those teachers who had "problems"—it was presumed that all teachers had erred by following the revisionist educational line. But we were careful not to mention the school leaders. Nobody dared to defend *them*.

I was very involved in the debate. When I made my argument, I had a specific teacher in mind—Teacher Wang. As a graduate of an American missionary school, she was a natural target. Since she was gentle and always soft spoken, I couldn't imagine treating her rudely. It was only reasonable to be kind and gentle in our treatment of teachers like her. For us the favorite quotation from Chairman Mao was *zhibing jiuren* (治病救人 / cure the illness and save the patient).

Soon it was clear to us that the political climate favored our opponents. Increasingly one heard the lines Mao wrote some 40 years ago about a peasant rebellion, which was now becoming the most authoritative definition of revolution:

> A revolution is not a dinner party, or writing an essay, or painting a picture, or doing embroidery; it cannot be so refined, so leisurely and gentle, so temperate, kind, courteous, restrained and magnanimous. A revolution is an insurrection, an act of violence by which one class overthrows another.[16]

The first time I witnessed violence was in July 1966, at a struggle meeting held at dusk in a gigantic stadium. In my mind that place resembled the Coliseum in Rome. The individuals targeted at the meeting were forced to stand on a temporarily built platform. The audience was secondary school students from all over Beijing. The meeting proceeded without much fanfare until suddenly some boys rushed down the stairs. They climbed onto the platform and began beating the men. I was shocked and shouted, "No beating!" It was an instinctive reaction. People around me also made the same protest. We were still able to express our objection, no matter how weak it was. Soon violence on a much larger scale broke out, but nobody dared to protest.

I will never forget the death of Bian Zhongyun, the party secretary and deputy principal of my school. She was beaten to death on the school campus by some students.

I had left school earlier that day with some classmates. When we returned, the beating was already over. I sensed something had gone wrong as soon as we arrived on campus. The first person we ran into was Teacher Wang. She looked scared and avoided any eye contact with us. Tall and a little bit hunchbacked, she bent down even further and edged along the wall as if trying to shrink into herself. Fear also was in the eyes of other people walking in our direction. I thought to myself, "Something has happened."

We learned that the whole episode was first started by some students from the first year of senior high. They ordered the school leaders to gather on the school sports ground, saying it was too comfortable for them to stay indoors. First the leaders were paraded around the campus. They were being cursed and beaten by a crowd of people following them, which now included students from other grades. Some used broken chair legs to beat them. Then a struggle meeting was held. More students had come out to watch. The leaders were told to stand on a high platform where they took turns denouncing themselves. Next they were told to transport dirt on the school sports ground. This was strenuous labor, and the weather was hot and humid. Bian Zhongyun could hardly move a step with the deliberately heavy dirt she was supposed to carry. For this she received lots of beating and cursing. At one point, I learned much later, she said to Hu Zhitao who was doing the physical labor next to her, "I can't do it. What shall I do?" This was probably her last words.[17] After the forced labor on the sports ground the leaders were assigned different tasks such as cleaning students' dormitory toilets. Throughout the whole time, physical torture and verbal abuse by some students never ceased. Finally Bian Zhongyun collapsed. She was then placed on a garbage cart and her blood-and-excrement-stained body was covered with used poster paper. A hospital was only a two-minute walk from our school, but nobody rushed her there. She was left lying in the cart for a long time. By the time she was finally taken to the hospital, it was too late.[18]

The next morning we all gathered in our classrooms to hear the school's daily broadcast. What came out from the loudspeaker was the following announcement: "Bian Zhongyun is dead. That is it. (死了就死了 / si le jiu si le) Don't mention it any more."[19] It was made by the head of the school's Student/Teacher Representative Committee, a group that now enjoyed greatly diminished prestige because of its association with the recently defunct work team, but it was nonetheless the only existing authoritative organization. The speaker's voice was flat and emotionless. I imaged that there was no expression on her face. After the brief statement the broadcast was over. But nobody in my class moved. We all sat in our seats and there was a deadly silence. This was the first time I experienced the death of a person I had known. What a death!

I had called Bian Zhongyun "Aunt Bian" in private because my parents knew her and her husband. A few months prior to the Cultural Revolution, my mother and I ran into Bian at a big department store near Wangfujing Street. She suggested that my mother buy me an expensive cashmere scarf, saying that it would make a nice dowry. I was surprised to hear this from a school leader. I had thought the leaders only concerned with big revolutionary ideas. I didn't like the bright colors of the scarf, but my mother went ahead and bought it anyway. After the Cultural Revolution began, anybody who dared to wear such a scarf would be accused of indulging in a bourgeois lifestyle. So the scarf stayed at the bottom of a trunk. I saw it again many years later. The colors had faded and there were tiny moth holes all over; it reminded me of Aunt Bian.

Nobody has claimed responsibility for Bian's death. Her husband, who is now in his eighties, has waited for an apology all these years, but no one from my school has yet come forward.

Other leaders were also badly beaten that day. The dean of the school had a broken spine and was hospitalized for a long time. Hu Zhitao, the deputy principal, suffered severe pelvic bone damage. She had to lie in bed for weeks. Among her most eager persecutors, I am pretty sure, were cadres' children. At this early stage of the Cultural Revolution beating was the privilege of people from red families. The students must have been Hu's audience at a meeting she chaired especially for cadres' children prior to the Cultural Revolution. I couldn't help think about the irony.

Hu Zhitao's demeanor during the Cultural Revolution greatly impressed me. She became the prime target after the death of Bian Zhongyun and was abused whenever students felt like it. But she always held her head high and walked with poise, despite the fact that she had to wear a metal vest to protect her broken ribs—another result of the student beating that day.

Soon after the beatings at my school, violence erupted in my parents' work unit. This time I heard the violence, though again I was not present. On August 10, some rebels at Xinhua paraded a large number of individuals accused of being black gangsters around the compound. My family was then living in a courtyard just outside the compound. That day both my brother and I were home. Sometime in the early afternoon we heard harsh noises coming out of the compound. They were a mixture of shouting, yelling, and screaming. It was hard to believe that such barbarous sounding noise could come from a place where the people were highly educated. We joined some neighbors who had gathered in the yard. Among them there was a Czechoslovakian woman. She was married to a Chinese man and had lived many years in Beijing. She kept asking, "What is going on?" Her voice was shaking and her Chinese sounded even more broken than usual. Nobody knew what to say.

We later learned that more than one hundred men and women were put on parade that day. They included almost all the people holding responsible positions at Xinhua along with people with all kinds of political problems from the past. As the deputy head of a major department, my father was not spared. They were forced to wear dunce hats and heavy boards over their necks with their names crossed out in red ink.[20] As they walked in a circle under the hot August sun, they had to shout self-denouncing slogans and were beaten randomly by the rebels.

Nobody died as a direct result of the physical abuse. Later that day, however, two people committed suicide, a man and wife. I heard that when the couple returned home from the parade, what awaited them was a family struggle meeting conducted by their children. This was more than they could take. That night they both took their lives.

It was not uncommon for children to struggle against their parents. During the big Xinhua parade, for instance, a man was humiliated by his children, with his estranged wife watching and cheering. The older child was only about ten and the younger one no more than eight. I had been fond of them because of their doll-like faces. Now they followed their father and spat at him. Violence didn't have to be physical. Psychological torture could be even crueler, especially if it was done by your own children.

* * *

MA: My memories of August 1966 are blurred, as so many things happened in so short a time. But one event stands out. On August 18, Mao received representatives of the Red Guards on the balcony of Tiananmen. It was his first public appearance since the beginning of the Cultural Revolution. I went with the Red Guards in my school. I had recently joined the organization, which was automatically open to anyone from a red family. That day the Tiananmen Square turned into a sea of people. When Mao appeared, the young students were screaming, jumping, and crying. I also cried and thought I was the happiest person in the world.

YE: I also became a member of my school's Red Guards simply because of my family background. I don't recall when and how I joined. The whole thing was very informal. On August 18 students of my school also went to the Tiananmen Square. But I don't remember the frantic scene. We had to gather at three o'clock in the morning to walk to the square. When we got there, it was still dark. I was so sleepy that I just sat down and fell asleep. At dawn I vaguely heard some students' names being called. They ended up on the balcony of Tiananmen and later had pictures taken with Mao and other top leaders.

I knew somebody who was on the balcony that day and got to shake hands with Mao. Afterwards she didn't wash her hands for quite some time so that other people could touch them and share her happiness. I sometimes wonder if I had shaken hands with Mao would that experience have transformed me into a more enthusiastic participant of the Cultural Revolution? I suppose personal encounters with larger-than-life figures like Mao could produce miraculous effects.

MA: What has stuck to my mind is a photo that appeared the next day in the paper. It showed your school's Song Binbin putting the Red Guard band around Mao's arm. Mao asked about Song's name. When he learned that her name was Binbin, which means "gentle," he said, "*yaowu ma.*" (要武嘛 / be militant).

YE: This was taken as a message Mao gave to all the young people. Soon afterward even my school's name was changed to The Red Militant School. By donning an army uniform, Mao conveyed the impression that this was a war-like situation and he was the commander-in-chief. Mao's public appearance strongly bolstered the Red Guard movement.

The Anti-four-olds Campaign (against old customs, habits, culture, and thinking) was launched right afterward. *Da, za, qiang* (打砸枪 / beating, smashing, and seizing) became commonplace. This made August remembered as the month of "red terror." In late August a second person was beaten to death on my school campus. The victim was a young waitress working in a neighborhood restaurant. Accused of being a loose woman, she was brought over by Red Guards from a nearby boys' school to be "taught a lesson" by female Red Guards in my school. She was only eighteen. Police statistics show that this short period witnessed the peak of violent deaths in Beijing.[21] I can support the report with a personal observation. I noticed around this time an unusual type of black vehicle in the streets. One afternoon I stood by the Chang'an Boulevard and saw several of them passing by within a short time. I later found out that these peculiar-looking vans were used by the Beijing crematorium to transport corpses.

Violence even occurred among classmates. One day a cadre's child in my class slapped a girl in the face and knocked her glasses to the floor. The girl had acted defiantly despite her black family background. Everybody was shocked by the scene, but nobody dared to say a word.

I am still puzzled by why our generation was capable of committing violence. Before the Cultural Revolution we saw violence such as torturing only in movies. It was always done by the enemy to revolutionaries—so it was unacceptable.

MA: But our education didn't teach us to oppose all violence. Counter-revolutionary violence was bad, but revolutionary violence was necessary. Violence was justified if it was against the class enemy. When the Cultural Revolution began, one could either be on the side of the revolutionaries or with the enemy—there was no middle ground. As a revolutionary you were supposed to be firm and tough-minded. There was no room for soft feelings. I tried very hard to eliminate my petty bourgeois sentiments. Whenever they came up, I would squelch them.

YE: You were striving to be a revolutionary. I found it hard to make myself into one. After the violent death of Bian Zhongyun I thought to myself, "If this is what a revolution is about, I cannot be a revolutionary."

MA: The subject of violence is difficult for me. I was present at two violent acts and took part in one of them. At first I was not very involved in my school's Red Guard activities. During the Anti-four-olds Campaign, I wandered around the neighborhood near my school, often times with a few class-mates. Many homes were being searched by Red Guards for evidence of four-olds as well as counter-revolutionary crimes.

Once we entered a house where a search was going on. The head of the family was a former capitalist. Inside a room stood four or five members of the family, all with their heads bent. Some male Red Guards were questioning them, asking each to report what his / her family background was. When they came to a middle-aged woman, she timidly replied, "Poor peasant." A Red Guard, who seemed to be the most ferocious in the group, snapped, "How could a poor peasant become the concubine of a capitalist?" So she was a concubine, something I thought had disappeared long ago. The boy went up and suddenly grabbed the woman's hair to look at her face. My heart shrank. I knew he wanted to see if she was good-looking. It was wicked and disgusting. The woman was trembling and her hair was a mess. She must have felt hurt. I quickly left.

But later I myself participated in a beating. One evening I heard some noise coming from a classroom on my school campus, so I went there to check it out. Several Red Guards from the upper classes were beating a fat woman in her forties. She wore a tight black outfit so her figure clearly showed. I disliked her at first sight. I asked about the reason for the beating. A girl whispered that the woman had cursed Chairman Mao. I couldn't believe my ears. How dare she! At that moment the woman said, "I did say Chairman Mao is a pig." Hearing this with my own ears, I was outraged and shouted back, "*You* are the pig!" Taking a belt from the hand of a girl nearby, I began to hit her. The belt made a strange "peng peng" sound. I didn't see any swelling or blood on her body. The woman kept writhing on the ground and screaming. I thought she was exaggerating and that made me even angrier, so I beat her harder. I left after a while. I don't know what eventually happened to her.

As I think about it now, I've come to realize that most likely the woman had lost her mind. Otherwise why did she keep saying things that could easily cause her death? I've asked myself numerous times if I could have behaved differently. For instance I could have suggested to the other Red Guards to let her go because she was mentally ill, or I could have just denounced her verbally. But I was too young to tell the difference between a political crime and a mental illness. I had neither the courage nor the maturity to behave differently. Besides, Mao's personality cult was at its peak. Anybody who dared insult Mao was inviting his / her own termination. Still, I cannot make peace with what I did that night. This is the first time I have ever talked about it with another person.

YE: But it sounds like you've given this incident a great deal of thought. Speaking of house searches, the first time I heard of a lesbian marriage was after some Red Guards from my school searched a home in a nearby alleyway. The tip came from the neighborhood committee. They told the Red Guards that a suspicious couple lived in their neighborhood. When Red Guards went to the house, they found two women living together. One always dressed in men's suits. The couple even had a wedding photo in which they posed as husband and wife. Later this photo and other evidence of a "sickening life style" were on display in the neighborhood to shame the two women. Soon afterward, a lesbian couple in my school was also exposed. They were both mathematics teachers of the highest rank and had enjoyed great respect before the Cultural Revolution. The rumor was that the two teachers shared the same bed. I knew nothing about homosexuality, but somehow I felt it was strange that two women were sleeping together.

MA: Now personal conduct was public business. I heard that a woman was humiliated because she had affairs with men. As a punishment she was forced to wear a string of worn shoes around her neck, the sign of a loose woman.

YE: Not just private conduct, but even personal issues like one's hairstyle were subject to public scrutiny. At the height of the Anti-four-olds Campaign, I went to Wangfujing Street with some classmates. We had heard that some Red Guards were taking down old shop signs and putting on revolutionary sounding new ones, so we went there to have a look. There we saw a crowd in front of a big store. In the center stood a woman with two long braids. Surrounding her were some male Red Guards and many onlookers. The Red Guards told the woman to cut off her braids or they would cut them for her. The braids infuriated the Red Guards because the notorious counter-revolutionary Deng Tuo had praised long hair in his essay.[22] Hearing their argument, I asked the boys, "What if Deng Tuo has also recommended drinking boiled water? Would that mean we should all stop drinking water?" While I was speaking, I felt someone pulling the edge of my shirt. I understood this person was telling me to stop. I wore a Red Guard armband, which was like an amulet in those days. Still, I realized this was not the place to make a public scene. So my friends and I quickly left. On our way back, we suggested to one girl among us to cut her braids. She did so soon.

My own family was searched several times by people from my father's department. Luckily I was never there when they came, but they seized my things. I mentioned to you earlier that I sketched nude women when I was about 13. The drawings were kept in a drawer in my bedroom and I never showed them to anyone. When those people came, they took my drawings with them. Later they displayed the drawings in my father's department to embarrass him, saying that the daughter's unhealthy thinking reflected the bad influence of the father. I felt acutely humiliated. How I wished to find a hole in the ground so that I could disappear from the world! I feared that at any moment my friends would find out, and I would be expelled from the Red Guards. My parents tried to make me feel it was not such a big deal. Then they dropped the subject. I guess they wanted to see the whole episode fade away.

During another search, my diary was taken. This time the consequences were more serious. My father's department labeled it counter-revolutionary and sent it to my school. It ended up in my dossier and followed me to the countryside. However, I didn't even know it was there until much later.

I Got to Know My Parents Better

As the situation turned increasingly chaotic I stopped going to school regularly and had a lot of time on my hands. I sometimes would venture into the work area of Xinhua to look at wall posters. Nobody would bother to stop me from entering. One day I spotted a poster with my father's name crossed out in red ink. The language was so rude that I hurriedly left after reading only the first few lines. I felt as if all the people there were pointing their fingers at me.

Once I was at a meeting where the main target was the head of Xinhua. My father and a few other department chiefs accompanied their director to this struggle meeting. I was nervous that violence might break out at any moment. Luckily the meeting was quite civilized by the standard of the day— no pushing, kicking, or bending the back in a "jet airplane" position. The people just stood on the stage of the auditorium with their heads lowered.

A lot of the Xinhua struggle meetings were held in the auditorium. I would sneak in occasionally and sit in a corner upstairs. I knew most of the people on the stage. They had held responsible positions at Xinhua before the Cultural Revolution and had been parental figures to me. Previously these people had personified the revolution in the eyes of young people like me, but the Cultural Revolution broke their halos. They behaved differently under fire. I admired those who were able to hold themselves together no matter how intense the pressure. There were others who were always ready to sell out their colleagues in exchange for better treatment. I despised them. I learned from the Xinhua struggle meetings how savagely some so-called intellectuals could behave. More than once I saw them beat people in broad daylight. I came to realize that education didn't necessarily make a person civilized and humane. I had grown up in the Xinhua compound and had always regarded the place as home, but the Cultural Revolution forever severed my emotional attachment to the compound.

My father was once kidnapped by an outside rebel organization. My mother and I looked for him all over the Xinhua compound. He returned home a few days later in terrible shape. He had been taken to a college campus in the suburbs and interrogated by college students there. They also beat him.

Since my father was now considered a black gangster, the kids in the streets constantly bullied my sister. After being spat at or having stones thrown at her, she often hid herself in a corner crying. She was barely seven years old. I only found out how terrible her situation was much later. At the time I was too engrossed in my own world to pay attention to my little sister.

My family remained close throughout this turbulent time. The Cultural Revolution did not change our relationships with our relatives either. Almost every relative's family was in trouble. For a while my third and fifth paternal uncles were imprisoned in the notorious Qincheng Prison[23] for the same "counter-revolutionary crime" they had allegedly committed years ago,[24] and the two brothers didn't know they were in such close proximity. My third maternal uncle was ordered to return to the village of his birth where he had left years ago as a young man. Now in his sixties, he had to learn to support himself by farming.

I went to see my third paternal uncle Ye Duyi soon after his release from the Qincheng Prison where he ended up spending more than four years. He had lost so much weight that he looked like a human skeleton. I had never seen a thinner person in my life and the image scared me. There was no need to inquire what life was like in the prison. My uncle was a living (barely) testimony of its horrifying conditions. He later told us that he had managed to keep his sanity by mentally going over all the entries he could remember in an English dictionary from A to Z. Who would have expected that my uncle's incredible memory, famous among family members, was put to such use!

My uncle's French was also very good. Once, I think it was around 1974 or 1975, my brother and I were invited to his shabby home to listen to Victor Hugo's *Les Miserables*, told entirely from my uncle's memory of the novel he read years ago in original French. The story telling lasted for about two weeks. By following the adventure of Jean Val Jean (whose name was pronounced in a funny way by my uncle), my uncle took us on an imagined journey to nine-teenth-century France that somehow had the curious effect of transcending the ugly, oppressive politics of the day in China.

Compared with my third paternal uncle, my third maternal uncle Bai Jingyang was more of a traditional type Chinese scholar and he coped with the adversities in his life in a different way. In the later years of the Cultural Revolution my brother and I went to one uncle for English tutoring and the other for classical Chinese studies. Once to illustrate a line from a text of the Confucian school that read "a person should be able to shoulder the burden of great difficulty" ("大事难事者担当" / *dashi nanshi zhe dandang*), my uncle stood up and raised his arm as if to hold up something heavy. I was somewhat amused because he was tall and hunchbacked, his arm long and bony. This did not fit the conventional image of a hero. My uncle was then living in the countryside by himself and was only allowed to return to the city in wintertime. Was he using this line to encourage himself? With retrospect I now wonder. I sensed at the time that my uncle was able to derive moral strength from a source unfamiliar to me, which could be vaguely identified as Confucianism. It had been harshly treaded during the Cultural Revolution, but it helped my uncle retain his basic sense of human dignity.

My mother continued to help her brother's family financially. On my father's side, a cousin who was getting married asked my father, his uncle, to represent the family at his wedding since his parents had gone to a "cadres' school" (a labor camp in actuality) in a far away province. If anything, the Cultural Revolution brought my extended family even closer. But too often you heard of family members turning against each other. The only relative to turn against her family was the daughter of my first paternal uncle. She led a group of Red Guards from her school in Beijing to search the home of her own family in Tianjin. The Red Guards ordered *nainai*, my cousin's grandmother, to kneel on the ground. Shortly afterwards the old lady died. The rest of the family has never forgiven this cousin for what she did to *nainai*.

I got to know my parents better because of the Cultural Revolution. There is one scene that has been carved in my mind. It was after my father was publicly humiliated during the big parade at Xinhua. As soon as my parents came home that evening, my brother and I went up to them and asked, "What's going on?" We were both crying. Recent events at school and at Xinhua were simply too much. I saw my father's eyes turn red. This was the first time we had ever seen our father crying. It scared us so we cried even harder. At that moment I heard my mother say to my father, "Don't cry." I was stunned. My father stopped crying. So did my brother and I. For a while the four of us stood there as if we were all frozen. My mother had always been soft-spoken. I did not realize she could speak in such a commanding voice.

My parents differed in their attitudes toward China's predicament. At dinnertime they always had a half-serious / half-joking debate about the future of the country. My father thought China was finished and he sighed a lot. My mother would insist that there was hope. My father would say, "I don't see it. You are blindly optimistic." My mother would reply, "Then call me *mangle* (blind optimist)." So *mangle* became the nickname my mother gave herself. The nickname she gave my father was *nan'nan* (difficult, difficult). During my parents' dinner table debates, my brother and I just listened. We were also worried about the future—the country's and our own. Thanks to our mother's "blind optimism" we managed to survive the darkest period of the Cultural Revolution.

My mother began to treat me like a friend. After dinner we always took a walk together. My mother was lame so we walked slowly. At this hour there was hardly any traffic or people in the street. Under the dim streetlight were just the shadows of a mother and a daughter. My mother told me a lot about her past, especially her life during the war. Her calm demeanor, her refusal to give up hope, and her sense of humor were invaluable to me.

Three years or so into the Cultural Revolution, my mother found herself in serious political trouble. She had criticized Mao's wife, Jiang Qing, to an old friend, and this friend reported their private conversation to the authorities. My mother was accused of being a counter-revolutionary. Luckily she was not arrested, but her desk was moved to the hallway as a punishment and she was forced to make a humiliating public confession in the auditorium before the entire Xinhua community. By this time I had gone to the countryside. I felt terrible that I couldn't be by my mother's side when she was suffering.

"The Red Guards Cut Your Mother's Hair"

MA: In my family there wasn't much communication between parents and children, since my parents thought we were just kids. In my memory, the atmosphere at my home was already quite depressing prior to the Cultural Revolution. We stopped going to parks, cinemas, and restaurants. I don't think it was because my parents thought my brother and I were too old to take us out. I noticed some changes in my father. He looked tired. At the dinner table he seldom spoke. His mood affected everybody else. We all kept quiet and there was no joy at home. I missed the good old days my family used to have together.

Then the Cultural Revolution began. My father didn't suffer very much. As a middle-ranking cadre in his ministry he was not a primary target. But it was different for my mother, as she was the party secretary of a secondary girls' school. In the hectic days of August, I often stayed at school overnight and sometimes didn't go home for days. When I did go home, I could tell that things were not going well. My father often closed their bedroom door and my parents would whisper inside. Those days anybody who had held a responsible position before the Cultural Revolution could be under attack, so I knew my parents wouldn't be spared. But it never occurred to me that my mother would suffer greatly until one day in late August.

That day I happened to go home from school. As soon as I came through the door, my father grabbed my arm and took me aside. He said, "Mother's inside. The Red Guards in her school cut her hair. Be prepared when you go in." I was dumbfounded. Somehow I finally entered her room. Her hair was a total mess like a trampled lawn, cut roughly with scissors. They had given her a "yin / yang" haircut.[25] When my mother saw me, she began to cry. I also cried. My father stood there saying nothing. It must have been very painful for him.

It was obvious that my mother couldn't go out like this. People would be able to tell right away that she was a black gangster and she could be further humiliated. We couldn't find any store that sold hats for women, so my mother had to wear a man's cap. When winter came, my sister-in-law knitted a woolen scarf for her so that she wouldn't look so bad. It took more than half a year before she could go outdoors without a hat.

YE: I didn't realize your mother had suffered so much. Why did you wait until now to talk about it?

MA: It was too painful, not only because the subject itself was hard for me, but also because I only recently learned the details of that day. My father wrote an account soon after my mother's death in 1981 in which he described what happened in the summer of 1966. He only let me read it in 1998. This is what he wrote:

> Hewen [my mother's name] was forty-two in 1966. She was in the prime of her life, well educated, experienced at work and in good health. But then came the Cultural Revolution. Schools, especially secondary schools, were the first to be turned upside down. Hewen became a black gangster at her school. She was confronted at numerous meetings, where she was spat at, hit by stones, had her body bent in the "jet airplane" position and was forced to don a heavy board over her neck and a dunce hat on her head. She tried her very best to endure all these abuses.
>
> The worst finally came on August 24th when, at a meeting in the school, Hewen was severely beaten along with five other former leaders of the school. Two died on the spot. Hewen's life was spared, but her hair was shaved and wounds covered all her body. When she came back from school, all I could do was to clean the blood from her body. While dressing her wounds, I cried and asked myself why she had to suffer like this. I was afraid that after this horrendous experience Hewen would not want to live anymore. We stayed up the whole night and I tried my best to comfort her and to discourage any thought of suicide. Early the next morning, Hewen had to return to the school. I saw her off at the gate. Watching her walking haltingly away, I knew she was in great pain. I cried again. In the ensuing weeks she did heavy manual labor at school. Imagine a woman with a queer-looking haircut laboring under the public eye. Constantly mortified, Hewen defied adversity. It was not until late November that she was able to wear a scarf to cover her head. After this incident, Hewen was easily startled and would often wake up in the middle of the night. She also developed heart problems. It is not hard to understand why she would have cancer later in her life.

I felt terrible that I had not known the details of what happened that day. After the incident I didn't notice any change in my mother's demeanor and my father also seemed to behave normally. It was incredible how my parents were able to hide their pain from us children. I had never seen my father cry, so it broke my heart to read about his crying.

After the beating, we were nervously waiting for the Red Guards to come and search our home. My father warned us repeatedly not to confront them when they came. But they didn't come. Meanwhile, the people in the compound continued to treat my mother kindly, and nobody took advantage of this incident to abuse my brother and me.

I never doubted that my parents were good party members and I knew they were certainly not black gangsters. I constantly remembered what my father told us, "We should trust the masses. It's only natural that they may make mistakes. Allow for their mistakes." These words calmed me down.

YE: But how could you still trust the "masses" if they were capable of doing horrible things? I lost that trust.

MA: I thought the masses were wrong in the case of my parents, but I also knew that mistakes were inevitable in a big movement like the Cultural Revolution. I tried not to be angry even with those Red Guards in my mother's school.

YE: You were a lot more generous than I. I resented those individuals who had mistreated my parents.

MA: I never met the students who tortured my mother, and I didn't want to know who they were. What could I do about them? They were just teenagers. It is those who started the Cultural Revolution and encouraged the violence that should be blamed.

YE: But shouldn't the individuals who carried out the violence also shoulder some responsibility?

MA: I have chosen to put these matters out of my mind. Thinking about them would open up deep wounds. I cannot bear to watch any scenes in films or on TV that depict the brutality of the Cultural Revolution. My father is even worse. Whenever he sees a scene like that on TV, he will turn it off and leave the room.

In 1981 my mother died of cancer. In her last days she would sometimes murmur in her sleep. More than once I heard her talking about that August day when she was badly beaten. I then realized that horrible event had stayed with her all those years, even though she never talked to us about it again.

A year after my mother's death I gave birth to Niuniu. Since then my mother has always come to my dreams. Once I saw her emerging slowly from afar. Her face was vague but her voice was clear. In the end she said, "The dawn is here. I must go," and she faded away. When I woke up I thought to myself, "Isn't this *Hamlet!*" As a child I saw *Hamlet* both on stage and in film. I also read Shakespeare's play when I was older. The ghost of Hamlet's father and the conversation between father and son had left a deep impression on me and now often makes me think of my mother.

After my mother became a black gangster I had to withdraw from the Red Guards. The organization would not tolerate children of "ox ghosts and snake spirits" and I understood this was the rule. But the Red Guards in my class did not disdain me. To the contrary, they regretted that I could no longer be with them. I still remember the first time they left me behind. Standing on the second floor balcony, I watched my classmates gathering in the school-yard below. They looked up at me. There was no hostility in their eyes.

As I think about it now, how a person was treated by her classmates had a lot to do with the class leader. In my class, the leader was a girl who was politically more mature than most people her age. I remember a meeting she chaired. Before the meeting, she made it clear that no violence was allowed. And the meeting proceeded peacefully. There was a girl in my class whose father had participated in all the five anti-communist military campaigns in the 1930s as a Nationalist officer. If his daughter were in another class, she could have suffered tremendously and her father could easily have lost his life. My classmates did not assault each other as was the case in your class. We were fortunate to have a good leader.

*   *   *

After the stormy August 1966, things calmed down somewhat for us. In early fall of the same year, both of us rode the enormous tide of dachuanlian (大串联 / great linkup) to travel around the country. The great linkup was supposed to spread the revolutionary flame: Red Guards from Beijing were to carry revolutionary seeds to provincial cities, while students from the provinces were invited to the capital as "Chairman Mao's guests." After being received by Mao, they returned home zealous to make revolution. In reality, however, what the young students derived from this peculiar opportunity did not necessarily agree with the intended goal.

When both of us returned to Beijing from the great linkup in late fall, we found that the Cultural Revolution had entered a new phase. More old cadres had fallen into disgrace. A different kind of rebel organization had emerged, endorsed by the powerful Central Cultural Revolution Small Group led by Mao's wife Jiang Qing (hereafter Small Group).[26] Meanwhile the original Red Guards, resentful of the purge of their parents and bitter over their loss of revolutionary privilege, turned from the most ardent supporters of the Cultural Revolution into some of its most reckless opponents. At the same time, many ordinary citizens began dropping out of the movement, choosing to avoid increasingly senseless political conflicts. The chaotic situation opened up space for youngsters to create something of their own. A youth culture, or rather a counterculture, thus appeared, expressing itself in attitude, behavior, and lifestyle that were in sharp contrast with the ideals of the Cultural Revolution. An appreciation of this remarkable yet little studied phenomenon is important for an understanding of the paradoxes of the Cultural Revolution and its multifaceted human aspects.

I Felt Adrift

MA: I was bored and depressed after I left the Red Guards. I felt adrift. But soon *dachuanlian* (great linkup) began, and that gave me something to do. I was not yet sixteen and had never left Beijing. Now I could see the country. I was excited. It must sound totally bizarre to people today that young students could travel all over the country at no expense, receiving free room and board wherever they went. Travel arrangements were simple: I packed a few clothes, told my parents I was leaving, and off I went with a few classmates.

YE: I also left with a few classmates. I think it was sometime in September. When we got to the Beijing Railroad Station, we saw signs for various destinations set up in the big station square where a huge crowd of people gathered. We wanted to go to the furthest southern city a train could take us, so we lined up in front of "Guangzhou."

MA: I still remember how crowded the train was. People squeezed in wherever there was space, even under the seats and on the luggage racks, and the aisle was completely blocked. I twisted my body under a seat. When the train stopped at a station, people would hold out mugs from the windows and cry, "Water! Water!" Only strong young men would risk getting out of the train through the windows. We girls didn't dare do so even though we were dying for fresh air and water.

YE: Once our train stopped in the middle of nowhere for hours. Even though all the windows were open, the air quality was so bad that we felt suffocated. The great linkup brought chaos to the entire country and the railroad system was severely jeopardized. It truly fulfilled Mao's wish for *tian xia da luan* (天下大乱 / chaos under heaven).

The great linkup gave us some sense about the Chinese reality. In both Guangzhou and Changsha we noticed that women rather than men were doing heavy manual labor. I was amazed to see women driving huge horse carriages and pulling loaded carts. We also heard things unknown to us in Beijing. We learned that during the great famine in the early 1960s, many Guangzhou residents risked their lives trying to escape to Hong Kong.

MA: I didn't pay much attention to local life. All we did was go to school campuses to read wall posters and visit revolutionary relics. What made me very happy during the trip was being able to get a brand new military uniform from my uncle when I visited his family in Changsha.

YE: We also went to revolutionary relics. We paid a visit to Mao's family home in Shaoshan. I could tell his family was pretty well-off, probably a rich peasant, one of the five black categories. It then dawned on me why we had been told little about Mao's family except that it was "peasant," whereas we knew the exact class category of everybody else's family. It seemed that class analysis didn't apply to Mao.

In Guangzhou we went to the trade exhibition center. The products there were all for export. Many beautiful clothes were on display in the light industry hall. By the standard of the day, everything there—beautiful fabrics and well-tailored dresses on Western mannequins—represented a bourgeois life style. They offered a window into a world that seemed to have completely disappeared in Beijing after the Anti-four-olds Campaign. It was strange to find it still existing in this corner of Guangzhou. Not knowing how to deal with it, we walked through that hall as fast as we could and tried not to be tempted by the beautiful materials all about us.

* * *

MA: It was already late fall when I returned to Beijing from the great linkup. My memory is vague about what I did during this period. Much of it was simply killing time. Sometime in 1967 we were urged to go back to school. But there were no academic classes. All I remember is military drills being offered by soldiers of the People's Liberation Army (PLA).

The soldier in charge of my class was a tall slim man in his early twenties. He was a country boy, smart, nice, and very likeable. One day he taught us how to use a rifle. After he checked my position, he accidentally touched my face. He was embarrassed and his face turned the color of red cloth. I didn't feel offended. In fact, I liked his light touch.

YE: I don't remember the military drills, even though I'm sure my school must have had them. There wasn't a nice young soldier in my class to make it memorable.

With hindsight, I realize that the Cultural Revolution enhanced my puritanical tendencies. In Chinese culture the age of 18 is usually associated with sexual maturity for women. When people say "an eighteen-year old *big girl*," they are implying something. But the Cultural Revolution seemed to have condemned anything related to sexuality, so 18 became a shameful age. As I approached my eighteenth birthday I didn't feel any excitement. Instead I felt awkward. I found that my friends also felt the same way. We talked about our eighteenth birthday as if it were a despicable point in life.

My friends and I turned into "bystanders"(逍遥派 / *xiaoyaobai*) after we came back from the great linkup. We dropped out of the movement, seldom bothered to go to school and like you, did things just to kill time. I read whatever books I could lay my hands on. Luckily, our next-door neighbor had a big collection of Western literature. In the fall of 1966 this family moved to the suburbs, leaving their key to my parents. I spent hours in their dust-filled apartment reading books. It was fascinating to read Stefan Zweig's[27] "The Twenty-four hours in a Woman's Life" about a skillful gambler. Some people I knew were circulating Roman Rolland's[28] *Jean-Christophe*. The main character in this novel could easily be criticized as egocentric by the revolutionary standard of the day. But nobody cared. As a matter of fact, many people were attracted by his personality. There was now a change of mood among secondary school students, especially those original Red Guards. The Red Guard organization in my school seemed to have dissolved by this time.

MA: I also noticed the change. More and more original Red Guards stopped active participation in the movement when they suddenly realized the targets of the Cultural Revolution were none other than their parents. When I came back from the great linkup, I found the Red Guard organization in my school also was fading, as most of the girls had become children of the "ox ghosts and snake spirits." Now the Small Group supported a different group of rebels, many of whom had been regarded as "bastards' kids" by the original Red Guards.

YE: Many original Red Guards were resentful about the new political situation. Since it would be politically suicidal to directly blame Mao, they found fault with the Small Group headed by Jiang Qing, challenging its authority and implicitly questioning the premise of the Cultural Revolution. I identified with their resentment. But, at the same time, I was turned off by their obsession with birth-based privilege. Their trademark was the excessively long Red Guard armbands made of silk rather than the original cloth. They stopped wearing plain and simple old army uniforms and started to wear outlandish outfits. For girls it was long woolen scarves. For boys it was fur hats, high-quality leather boots, and well-tailored woolen army overcoats.

The irony was that the owners of the overcoats and boots were probably under attack as targets of the Cultural Revolution, while their children were having a field day. I guess this conspicuous display of social status helped compensate for the kids' endangered sense of superiority, as they had lost their privileged position in the revolution.

MA: I do remember seeing big crowds of young men and women dressed the way you describe, riding bicycles down the middle of streets, and deliberately blocking traffic. It was quite a scene.

YE: I was interested in watching these people. It seemed that certain compound youth-culture was on open display in the street. As most young people had stopped going to school regularly, they tended to hang around kids living in the same compound. It was the youngsters from a military rather than a civilian compound that were most likely to show off this way, as the political situation of their parents was not as badly affected as it was for the other kids. What amazed me the most was that some people began to embrace the very lifestyles they had fervently opposed only a few months ago.

MA: I heard that they partied a lot. *Lao mo* (老莫 / Old Moscow) was their favorite hanging-out place. It certainly was the most bourgeois restaurant in Beijing. It served Russian-style cuisine with fine china and silverware on the tables covered by ironed linen cloth. A former Red Guard invited her friends to Old Moscow for her birthday and wore a white gown for the occasion. The gown possibly was a trophy from a house search during the Anti-four-olds Campaign.

YE: Around this time some boys ranked girls according to their looks. A student in my school got a high score of 120 points, so she was simply referred to as "120 points" in some circles. And the girl, daughter of a high cadre, made no protest. This would have been unthinkable a few months ago. A widely circulated phrase among some boys was *pai bozi* (拍婆子), meaning "dating a girl" or more precisely "getting a girl."

MA: I was disgusted by this phrase. It sounded like the language of hooligans—so disrespectful of women.

YE: There also were those who got themselves into trouble in street fights or by committing minor crimes such as thievery and vandalism. Think about it, in a matter of just few months, the most revolutionary people at the beginning of the Cultural Revolution now stopped making revolution and started making trouble ... and even making love. The Culture Revolution surely produced surprises.[29]

* * *

MA: The most important thing I learned during the Cultural Revolution was that authority could collapse overnight. Nobody was infallible, not even the top leaders of the country. The world turned upside down in front of my eyes.

YE: If I were asked to describe the most familiar feeling I experienced during this stage of the Cultural Revolution, I'd have to say it was fear. The death of Bian Zhongyun certainly left a deep scar on my psyche. My fear intensified as the Cultural Revolution progressed. Since I harbored a lot of resentment against the movement, I couldn't help but vent my anger and frustration periodically. I would curse Jiang Qing and the Small Group loudly. My family now was left with only one room and the walls were very thin. After I let off steam, I would be seized by fear, afraid that some neighbor had heard me and would call the police. I would stay frozen for a while, waiting their arrival. When nobody appeared, I would take a deep breath and tell myself, "OK, I got away this time."

My parents had an old friend who once said to me, "Remember, everybody has a dossier.[30] Everything you do and every word you say that is improper will be kept on record and the dossier will follow you for the rest of your life." This prospect truly scared me. Then I came across a metaphor about an imaginary giant net. It was invisible, but no matter where you turned, you could not escape from it. This image of the net captured the state of my existence.

Ye's mother in the late 1930's. After the outbreak of the Sino-Japanese War.

上海迁泉
[相馆印章]

Ye's family picture in the 1950's. Her sister was not born yet.

Ye's family picture in 1984 during her first visit back to China after she came to study in the U.S.

Ye and a few other *zhiqing* from her village, taken during an outing to a nearby scenic mountain. Someone among them jokingly suggested they pretend to be "tourists from Australia."

Ye and her son, taken right before she left China in early 1981.

Ye's son finally joined Ye in the U.S. at about 6 years old. He was 12 in this photo.

Ye as a graduate student at Yale, taken in the mid-1980's.

王瓦 东方红 照大

Ma Xiaodong as a little girl.

Ma's family picture in the 1950s. Her elder brother is missing from the picture.

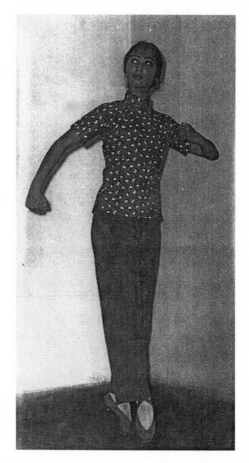

Ma was playing Quinghua, the heroine in the revolutionary ballet "The Red Detachment of Women" (in Yunnan).

Ma and her friends on the farm (in Yunnan).

Ma with children at an elementary school in Lexington, MA. Where she taught part time Chinese language and crafts.

Up to the Mountains, Down to the Countryside

Between the summer of 1968 and the spring of 1969, a large number of people in our age cohort left cities to go to various parts of the countryside.[1] Because of this shared fate, we acquired a collective name, "zhiqing" (知青 / educated youth), even though a secondary school student could hardly be qualified as educated. The term came from Mao's celebrated directive issued in December 1968: "It is necessary for educated youth to go to the countryside to receive re-education from the poor and lower-middle peasants."

The origin of the "up to the mountains, down to the countryside" movement can be traced to the mid-1950s when it first appeared as a way of solving the unemployment problem for surplus secondary school graduates. From the very beginning it was wrapped in high-sounding revolutionary rhetoric: educated youth should go to the countryside to help transform the backwardness of rural and frontier China. But it stayed small-scale and sporadic until 1968 when it evolved into a massive and systematic enterprise. By this time the political usefulness of secondary school students had been exhausted in the eyes of the Cultural Revolution leaders, and many of the youngsters had become dangerously restless. The movement offered a politically correct and economically plausible solution to a troubling situation. Mao's personal endorsement fueled the movement with great momentum. The notion of reeducation reflected Mao's dissatisfaction with the behavior of young people at this time. It also was consistent with Mao's long-standing criticism of the conventional educational system and his belief that the smartest people are those with practical knowledge.

To grasp the practical implications of the movement, some understanding of the Chinese residence registration system is needed. Once a person gave up her urban residence card, which was required of all the sent-down youth, she relinquished legitimate residence in the city she had lived, and it was well understood that once you lost that privileged status it was nearly impossibly to get it back. Given the huge gap between urban and rural China, this was a serious matter. Almost every zhiqing had a story about how he or she eventually regained the precious urban residence.[2] A small number has never been able to return to the city.

We left Beijing around the same time. Ma Xiaodong went to a state farm in Yunnan province while I settled in a village in northern Shanxi. State farms and rural villages represented two common destinations for educated youth, each with its distinct features. Both of us were struck, however, by how poor our respective destination was. The disparity between rural and urban China is an intriguing subject in its own right. It could be said that the large-scale "up to the mountains down to the countryside" movement during the Cultural Revolution bespoke an attempt to bridge the gap, though with hardly any sustainable results.

We belong to a generation that was born in urban China but largely came of age in the rural areas, thanks to our experience in the countryside. Since the 1980s a heated debate has been going on among the former zhiqing on whether or not it was regrettable for us to spend our precious youth as unskilled agricultural laborers. There is no simple and easy answer to this emotion-ridden question. Suffice it to say that no matter how each individual former zhiqing feels about this peculiar experience, "zhiqing" has remained a label, a memory, and an identity for an entire generation.

I Was a Five *Baozi* Girl: Ma Xiaodong's Story

"This is the Beginning of a New Life"

MA: A girl from my class left for the Great Northern Wilderness in Heilonggiang province in the summer of 1968. I had read books and seen films about the 1950s settlers who combated tremendous adversity there, turning virgin soil into profitable farmland. I yearned for a taste of frontier life myself. Hearing of my classmate's departure I thought that, if she went to the Great Northern Wilderness, I would go even further—how about Tibet! For a while I was obsessed with this thought, inquiring everywhere if Tibet needed young people from Beijing.

Then I learned that state farms in the southwestern province of Yunnan were recruiting students from Beijing. Since that province bordered Vietnam, it required strict political qualifications to go. I signed up immediately. By this time my father's problem had been resolved and my mother's situation had also improved, so my own political standing was strong. In the end I was one of the only two students in my class chosen to go. You can imagine how excited I was. Even though Yunnan was not Tibet, it was far enough. Besides, the name of my destination, Xishuangbanna, sounded delightfully charming. Life in Beijing had become so boring that I seemed to have lost a sense of purpose. Going to Yunnan offered me an opportunity to start anew.

We were not the first batch of Beijing youth to go to Yunnan. A year earlier 55 students from a number of Beijing secondary schools had already gone there. In fact, Premier Zhou Enlai personally approved their journey. They constituted one of the earliest groups of Beijing youth to voluntarily leave the city for the countryside. We followed in their footsteps. There must have been several hundreds of young people in our group. It was much larger than the first batch.

Between going to a village and to a state farm, my choice definitely was state farm. Living among country folk held no appeal for me. I had been to the countryside so I had some idea about peasant life. There the men worked in the fields from sunrise to sunset, while the women circled around stove and children. The very thought of living such a life depressed me. On a state farm I would be with people of my own age. We would work hard to build up the frontier. We also would have fun together. Life would be more exciting.

We left Beijing in November of 1968. The day before the departure, I opened the luggage my mother had packed for me to see what was there. I spotted a bag of candies. Immediately I threw it out, protesting to my mother, "No, no, I don't need candies. I am going to the frontier to live a plain and simple life. What would people think of me if they see me with these candies!" Before I realized what had happened, my mother grabbed the bag, put it back and pressed her whole body against the luggage so that I wouldn't be able to take the candies out. Tears were streaming from her eyes. I was taken aback. I didn't expect her to react so strongly to a bag of candies.

The day I left, the Beijing railway station was a sea of red flags and the atmosphere was quite festive. My friends all came to see me off. My parents were also in the crowd. They would face an empty nest now that I was leaving since my two brothers had already left home. How sad my parents must have felt. But I was not thinking about them at the moment. I was too excited. Some people were crying. Not me. I was chatting happily with friends. Suddenly I felt a violent shake. The train let out a long whistle and was about to move. The volume of crying suddenly increased. I stretched my arm out of the window and grasped my friends' hands tightly. I also cried. My parents were unable to squeeze to the front. My father was waving to me some distance away. He managed to compose himself, but my mother's eyes were all red. She was leaning against my father's tall shoulders like a sick person. I will never forget this scene.

We calmed down soon after the train left the station. Many people took out food to eat. I thought to myself, "So everybody has brought goodies along!" If my mother had not insisted, I would have had nothing for myself.

The train ride was memorable. On top of everything else, I spent my eighteenth birthday on that train. When the day arrived, our train was passing through central China. That morning I said to myself, "Today you are eighteen. This is the beginning of a new life for you." But I only celebrated the birthday in my heart. I made the pledge that I would work very hard to toughen myself in the countryside.

The train ride from Beijing to Kunming lasted three full days. It took us another four days to get to our final destination Xishuangbanna, first by bus and then by truck—a total of seven days. I guess it satisfied my desire to go as far as possible from home.

The farm had already prepared for our arrival. Rows of new houses, or to be precise, new huts, were waiting for us. Since we were organized in a semi-military fashion, each squad was assigned to a dorm. Standing inside a room, we could see the outside through the cracks in the bamboo walls and could hear conversations in the next room. The beds were also made of bamboo. On the first day a bed collapsed in the middle of the night and the noise woke everybody up. When we realized what happened, we all laughed. Next morning my clothes felt damp when I put them on. Looking outside I saw the morning air thick and white. I asked, "Did it rain last night?" Someone explained that humidity made the clothes wet. Was it always going to be like this? My heart sank. But eventually I got used to the weather there.

Because the weather was warm and humid even in winter, clothes molded all the time. The beautiful scenery around us, however, compensated for the weather. Every Sunday we went to a stream nearby to wash our clothes in crystal clear water. The mountains also gave us joy. Once we climbed to the top of a mountain and found ourselves surrounded by thick moving clouds. One minute everything was hidden in the clouds, the next the world reemerged in front of our eyes. We stirred the clouds and grasped them in our hands. It was even more extraordinary when we walked down the hill. We looked up and saw a magnificent scene. The sun was like a red ball, slowly setting behind the mountain ranges on the horizon. We cried out in one voice a line from a well-known poem by Chairman Mao, "The green mountains are like a vast sea and the setting sun is bloodily red!"[3]

Compared with humidity, miasma posed a more serious problem, because it could cause diarrhea. Once infected a person might not have enough energy to even sit up. Sometimes the entire company fell sick. But I was not dispirited. Didn't I come to Yunnan to taste hardship? I was eager and ready to temper myself.

At the first meeting upon our arrival the head of the company, a veteran state farm worker, said that two people were needed to work in the company kitchen. Any volunteers? Nobody in the audience raised a hand. People probably were thinking that we had come all the way from Beijing to build up the frontier, not to work in a kitchen. There was a long silence. Then I raised my hand.

YE: Did you know how to cook?

MA: No, I never cooked at home. I thought my problem in the past was that I was too eager to shine. Now was the time for me to learn to be a revolutionary bolt. Another girl, Jing, also raised her hand. We would become best friends.

I had to walk down a steep dirt path from my dorm to the kitchen. The road was always slippery because of constant rain. To prepare breakfast we had to get up at three o'clock in the morning when it was completely dark. Even with a flashlight I barely could see my way. It was deadly quiet and I felt like a ghost in the darkness. In a letter to my parents I told them about this experience. It was sort of boasting, like "See, how brave I am." Years later my father told me that, after they received the letter, my mother would wake up at three o'clock every morning. She would then say to my father, "Our daughter is now cooking breakfast." Learning this, I suddenly realized how stupid I had been. I had no idea this letter had caused my mother so much anxiety.

Cooking itself was simple. Everyday we had the same menu for the main meal: rice and a vegetable dish. For a while there was a shortage of grain. Girls were asked to eat less so that boys could have a little more. Jing and I decided we would only eat porridge for lunch. Every morning we put some leftover porridge from breakfast into two bowls. By lunchtime the liquid porridge would have turned into a solid mass. We were cheating ourselves since the amount of rice was the same—it only looked more. Soon we felt hungry again.

YE: Wasn't this what your friend Fan Lili's family did during the famine years?
MA: You're right. Perhaps that was where the idea came from. Sometimes we were also low on vegetables and cooking oil. Then we just boiled a big pot of thin soup with only a few vegetable leaves in it to go with the rice. One day I accidentally cut my middle finger while chopping vegetables, and a tiny bit of flesh was missing. That evening somebody announced that he had found a little meat in his supper. I thought it must be my finger, but I didn't say a word.
YE: I'm surprised that you didn't have enough food on a state farm. I thought this was only a problem for us in the villages.
MA: The food shortage didn't last long, but it left a deep impression on me. Even after we had a sufficient supply of grain and vegetables, there was hardly any meat. How we longed for a good meal! Our favorite pastime was to talk about the delicious food we used to have in Beijing. There was a small restaurant in a town 30 *li* away. We would walk all the way there just to have a nice meal. It took us a total of seven hours for the round trip. This was how we spent some of our Sundays. The scenery along the road was beautiful so we didn't mind the walking. The restaurant served salt-preserved meat and it was 30 *fen* a dish. See, I still remember the price. My monthly salary was 28 *yuan*. Besides 9 *yuan* to cover the food at the company canteen, the only expenses I had were occasional meals at local restaurants.

Part of our job was to purchase rice and vegetables in nearby villages. To carry the food back to the farm was a challenge. The local way was to tie the heavy bundle with a piece of cloth belt, place the bundle on the back, and then wear the cloth belt across the forehead. At first I couldn't do it. My head felt as if it were going to explode. But I was determined to master the skill. To test myself, I even walked with bare feet while carrying the weight on my head. Eventually I was able to walk for seven or eight *li* without a break, and this earned me the nickname, the barefoot immortal.

My grocery trips allowed me to see how the local people lived. One day we ran into a peasant man carrying an old woman on his back. The woman looked like a skeleton covered only by skin. It was shocking to see a human being this thin. The man told us they had come down the mountain and he was taking his mother to a doctor. To my knowledge there wasn't a hospital in the area. He must have been talking about the clinic at our state farm headquarters where only very basic medical treatment was available. Before I came to the countryside I had read about the great shortage of doctors and medicines in rural areas. Now I saw it for real.

Once I visited the home of a local woman. Her hut was made of bamboo. Inside it was covered with thick dirt so no light could come through. When I first entered the room my eyes couldn't make out anything even though it was daytime. I felt I was in a tomb. It took me quite a while to see the simple furniture right in front of me. A main staple in the diet of the local people was *bajiao* (芭蕉). It tasted like banana and was often cooked with rice. It might sound delicious but, like sweet potatoes, *bajiao* could cause stomachache if you ate too much of it, yet the villagers ate it everyday.

I resented those Beijing youth who refused to adjust to local living conditions. Once I spent a night with a few Beijing youth at an inn for traveling peasants. The bed sheets were so dirty that it was hard to tell what color they originally had been. A girl stayed up all night rather than sleeping in her bed. I thought, "Why are you so picky?" and went right ahead to sleep. On another occasion, we girls went to a stream to wash our hair. The water must have contained certain chemicals to make hair smooth and shiny. On our walk back to the dorms a truck passed by. It stirred up so much dust that our hair immediately got dirty again. A girl covered up her head and hurriedly ran away. I was annoyed by what she was doing.

YE: But she just tried to protect her hair from the dust.

MA: I agree with you now, but I didn't see it that way then. I thought that she was afraid of getting dirty. Who tended to look dirty? It was the laboring people, the peasants. This was what Chairman Mao said about them: "They have dirt on their hands and cow shit on their feet, but they are really the cleanest people in the world." We shouldn't look down upon them and should try to live like the peasants.

YE: You really tried hard to reform yourself. Did you work in the kitchen all those years?

MA: No, Jing and I left the kitchen after six months to work in a regular production team. Our job was to plant cinchona. From its bark quinine can be extracted. It would take five years before a young tree became useful, and only a tiny amount of quinine could be extracted from a large quantity of bark. But none of the trees we planted ever produced any quinine. It was because we left the region after a year and abandoned the trees. So our labor was totally wasted. On top of this, the original vegetation was also destroyed, because we had to clear the land before we planted cinchona trees.

But at the time we were totally ignorant about ecology. We only competed with each other to see who could plant more trees. When I heard that the best male worker was able to dig 50 tree holes a day, I decided I could do that too. To do so meant not wasting any movement. I mastered the skill and was able to dig a hole in just a few minutes. Jing too could do it. We two set the record of 50 holes a day for girls.

YE: Were you inspired by the "iron girl" (铁姑娘 / *tie guniang*) ideal?

MA: Yes. We wanted to prove "whatever men comrades can do, women comrades can do too."[4] Our fellow workers noticed what Jing and I were able to accomplish. One day we had *baozi* (包子 / meat-filled steamed buns) for lunch, which was a rare treat. There was a limit on how many *baozi* each person could have: for boys it was five; for girls it was four. Several boys suggested that Jing and I should also get five. I was very pleased. It was not about one more *baozi*, but the recognition of our hard labor. We had proved ourselves.

But it was hard to keep up the high pace. After a while everybody got tired. You could tell it by the way people reacted to different whistles. When the break whistle was blown, we rushed into the bushes and collapsed on the ground. When it was time to go back to work, we slowly got up and dragged ourselves out of the shade. Each step was an effort.

I did a radical thing then. I tried to prove it was possible to eliminate physical differences between men and women. Most of the girls would rest for a day or two when they had period. I thought it was unnecessary. I decided not to let anybody know when my period came. Since there was no privacy in the girls' lavatory, this was difficult to do but I was determined. I chose to go to the toilet only when it was dark or when there were few people around. For a while nobody seemed to notice my little secret. Then one day a girl asked, "How come I've never seen you have your period?" I gave her a smile but said nothing. Even with my period I would still carry heavy loads on my shoulders and walk the mountain roads for 20 or 30 *li* without a break. I was too young to know how to take care of my body. Once I had my period when we went to work in a rice paddy field. It was early in the morning and the water was icy cold. I hesitated for a second and then jumped into the chilly water, barefooted.

There was another episode in a different context. It was during the aftermath of a pretty severe earthquake. We were all sleeping outdoors in tents. One night a girl woke up to see a man standing in front of her bed. She screamed and the man ran away. The girls were all terrified. I thought, "Why makes such a big fuss? What's there to be afraid of?" When I went back to my tent that evening, I found the other girls had all moved their mosquito nets back to the huts, leaving only mine standing alone in the tent. I was annoyed and told myself, "I will sleep here by myself tonight. I will see who dares to come!" I hardly closed my eyes that whole night. I was really scared, but I was also angry, "Why do we girls have to be so frightened?" The next day, however, I moved back to the hut.

The Years in Simao

In our second year in Yunnan, our farm was placed under military leadership. We didn't become PLA soldiers, but the leaders above the company level were PLA officers on active duty. I had always wanted to join the military and now my dream was half fulfilled. I was overjoyed. We moved to a new place called Simao. There was a lake nearby. The beauty of the lake thrilled me. I had brought a camera from Beijing so I would sometimes go there to take pictures.

YE: Wasn't it "petty bourgeois" to do so?

MA: I couldn't help it. The scenery was simply captivating. The lake was surrounded by lush vegetation, so the reflection made the water look green. Some boys in our company made up a jingle: "The waves of the lake are green, but the faces of the soldiers on the military farms are even greener," meaning that we all suffered from malnutrition.

YE: If somebody took it seriously, the boys could have gotten themselves into political trouble, accused of "tarnishing the 'up to the mountains and down to the countryside movement.' "

MA: I know. But the political atmosphere was more relaxed now. People simply had a good laugh. As a matter of fact, our food situation had improved a lot since we moved to Simao. Simao was the site of the prefecture government and a big town. It had a main street with shops and restaurants, so we no longer needed to walk 60 *li* of mountain road to eat a good meal. Besides, we were living in brick houses. Bamboo huts were history. Our task now was to take care of tea bushes on the mountains. It was much lighter labor than planting cinchona trees. Nobody mentioned the poor cinchona trees anymore. They were forgotten.

I was in Yunnan for a total of five years, but I only worked as a full-time manual laborer for one year. After that I worked in the regiment performing art troupe. Our job was to perform for the employees on the military farm and the PLA troops stationed in the vicinity. We spent half the day working in the tea fields and the other half rehearsing songs and dances.

YE: You know, in those days the reputation of a performing art troupe was that it consisted of a bunch of lazy people who tried to avoid hard labor by doing easy stuff like singing and dancing.

MA: I know. That was a common impression. But our life was not really easy either. Rehearsal was intense work. You could loaf in the fields all morning but you could hardly snatch a moment's rest during an afternoon rehearsal. You were always expected to be in high spirits. It was exhausting.

Performances always took place in the evening. There was little entertainment those days so we were often treated as distinguished guests by our hosts. When we performed for a military unit, we were often treated with a nice meal. Although the food at our company canteen was much better now, there was still little meat. To be honest, we were all looking forward to a good meal at the end of the performance. Sometimes the complimentary meal concisted of as many as seven or eight dishes, and after a while we sort of took the good food for granted. One day we performed for an army unit in Simao. Our performance that night was below par. Afterward a troupe member overheard some soldiers say, "What a poor performance! All they cared about was the meal!"

When I learned what the soldiers had said, I felt deeply insulted. Without telling anybody, I decided not to eat any meals provided by our hosts. When everybody was busy eating, I would steal from the room and find a quiet corner to sit down. After a while I would quietly return to my seat and nobody would have noticed my absence. It was tough. My stomach would make noises and I tried my very best not to look at the food on the table.

YE: You ate nothing at all?

MA: When I returned to the dorm I would go to Jing. She knew my secret and had kept some leftover supper for me from the canteen. I did this six or seven times, and only stopped when somebody found out.

YE: You were amazing. I couldn't do what you did. Besides work, was there anything else going on in your life? . . . Any romance?

MA: I noticed a tall boy in the performing art troupe. We were partners in a dance. In one act he was supposed to hold my hand. It was nothing unusual for men and women to hold hands during performances. But it felt different with him. I was sort of waiting for that moment to come, and I could tell he was also nervous. I told Jing how I felt. She said, "Why don't you tell him?" I couldn't do it. Love was an unknown thing to me. Somehow I felt that love and revolution were incompatible.

YE: Gadfly and Paul were your heroes. Didn't they both have lovers?

MA: True; but on the other hand, neither of them had a fulfilling love life. I longed for love, but I didn't know where it would take me. I definitely did not want marriage. At that time I thought I would remain single for the rest of my life. I guess my fear for marriage had something to do with a local girl who used to work at the company kitchen with us. She was very pretty. When

I first saw her, I was surprised to find such a good-looking girl in this poor mountain region. She was a member of Lisu, a minority nationality. She had a lively personality and was very smart. She taught us how to cook. Otherwise how would somebody like me know what to do in a kitchen? We were all fond of her and we had a lot of fun together. But she didn't stay with us long. After getting married she quit her job and we lost contact. About two years later I spotted her in a passing truck in Simao. I was startled. She had aged so much! It was clear that life hadn't been easy for her. When she was with us she was full of life and her laughter always accompanied our work. Now she looked worn out. I saw how marriage could ruin a woman. Was I going to be like her? This thought tormented me for a long time. I told myself I would never take the same path. I was determined to avoid the trap so many women had fallen into.

YE: But it was tough to keep this promise at our age. Besides that boy, did you have any other romantic involvement around this time?

MA: Well . . . something happened that I seldom tell other people. It was after the earthquake when we moved back inside the huts. Some of the huts were damaged so we had to squeeze into a few good ones. Because of the limited space we had to share beds. I shared mine with Jing. You know that it was not unusual for Chinese women to share beds. One night I woke up and found Jing missing. Where could she be at this hour? I went out to look for her but didn't see her anywhere. I became worried and reported her absence to the company leader. The leader and another man went out to search for her. After a while they brought her back. She had been sitting by herself somewhere outdoor. I asked her why. She said, "I always fear that I might lose you." I was puzzled. Weren't we together everyday? She replied, "You don't understand."

Later, she wrote about this to her mother. Her mother's response was calm and rational. She told Jing that she was probably experiencing homosexual love. This was understandable in an environment where there was not much contact between men and women. She predicted that this phase would pass and she hoped that Jing and I would remain friends. Jing's mother was a staff editor at a youth magazine in Beijing and must have encountered similar cases in her work, so she knew how to handle the situation sensibly. Jing showed me the letter and it helped ease the shock and discomfort I was feeling. Jing was a dignified person and she never approached me inappropriately. We continued to be good friends. A few years later, we both left Yunnan. Jing fell in love with a man in college and is now happily married.

YE: So there wasn't much contact between the sexes on the farm?

MA: At first boys and girls didn't mingle much, even though we worked side by side. Our job was to toughen ourselves through physical labor. Any other thoughts were inappropriate. Eventually things loosened up. I began to hear rumors, such as a boy was approaching a girl. A girl I knew received a love note from a boy. She was very upset and handed the note to the leaders. Soon everybody knew about it and the boy was humiliated. This incident led to a debate among us. Some thought the girl had done the right thing. Others contended that it was wrong to have reported the matter to the authorities. If the girl was not interested in the relationship, she should have told the boy directly. I agreed with the latter opinion.

One day we were all taken by surprise when we heard that a Beijing girl was going to marry a local man. Nobody was aware that the two had even been dating. The company gave them a nice wedding party, and the girl moved out of her dorm to a room assigned to them by the company. Thereafter they ate by themselves and the girl even raised a few chickens, just like the local women. The whole thing left me wondering if marriage was always this mundane.

Then we heard something truly shocking. Our company leader, a PLA officer, was caught having an affair with a girl from Beijing. The man had been a good leader. People cursed both the man and the girl, but especially the girl. She was blamed for seducing the company leader. After the incident, he had to retire from the military and return to his home village. The girl also disappeared and we heard she had an abortion. Later we learned that the man had divorced his wife and was planning to marry the girl. So theirs was a serious relationship.

Because ours was a military farm, we pretty much followed the routine set up for us. On Sundays we would either go eat in a restaurant, or go to the shops in town—mostly for window-shopping—or to see films. There were only a few politically correct films available, such as "Lenin in 1918" and the film adaptations of the "model plays,"[5] and we saw them again and again. There were few books available as none of us had brought any novels from Beijing. What we did read were works by Marx, Engles, and Lenin and we read them at our political study sessions, which we held once a week.

One thing I treasure very much about my life in Yunnan was friendships. I made some of my best friends there. My closest friend was Jing. Jing's father was a rightist, but this didn't bother me. Jing was not much older than I, but she always treated me like a big sister. Some girls thought I was too radical when they learned that I was hiding my period, but Jing understood me. I still feel proud after so many years that together we set the record of digging

50 tree holes a day, proving that girls were physically as capable as boys. Besides Jing there were two other girls with whom I was very close. We did things together, shared each other's secrets and gave each other support. Because of these friendships, I was never homesick. When I was away from the farm, I would miss my friends terribly. In one letter to them I wrote, "I miss all of you. I really want to tell you, 'I love you!' " They laughed at the word "love" and thought it sounded too petty bourgeois. I have to say Yunnan revitalized my romanticism and idealism.

But even so, questions began to come to my mind as time went by. When we first arrived in Yunnan, I thought I would settle there for the rest of my life, but eventually people around me began to leave, one after another. I debated intensely with myself. Would I betray my ideals if I return to the city? But what were my ideals anyway? To realize communism? What was communism? I realized that I didn't really know. To change the backwardness of the countryside? The task was too daunting for any individual. To integrate with the peasants? What did that mean? Marrying a local person and having lots of children? That would be my worst nightmare. The more I thought, the more confused I became.

On September 13, 1971, the Lin Biao Incident happened.[6] I was totally shocked. The incident further deepened my confusion. Chairman Mao's handpicked successor betrayed him and even wanted to kill him! My trust in many things suddenly turned shaky. It was like you had been walking firmly toward a goal and felt good about it. Then one day you found out that the goal was only an illusion. I felt terribly lost. I was scared that I might lose direction in life.

The Lin Biao Incident enhanced my doubts about staying in Yunnan. I began to think seriously about leaving.

A Tale of Two Worlds: Ye Weili's Story

Anybody can Be a Peasant

YE: A month or so after your departure to Yunnan, I also left Beijing. My destination was a village in northern Shanxi, near Inner Mongolia. I had been to the Beijing train station many times to see friends off. Now it was my turn. I didn't see many excited faces in the crowd even though the drummers' noise was deafening amid a waving field of red flags. I think there was a change of mood now from when you left. Early on people voluntarily signed up to go. Now we didn't have a choice. A few days earlier Mao personally endorsed the "up to the mountains and down to the countryside" movement. Except for an only child or people with health problems, almost everybody in our age group had to go.

I didn't mind leaving Beijing. Most of my friends had already left for either the Great Northern Wilderness or the grasslands in Inner Mongolia. If going to the countryside was the only option open to us, there was no point in delaying my own departure. I decided to go to a village rather than a state farm, even though going to a state farm meant more political prestige and economic security. We all knew that a state farm worker earned a regular salary whereas the income of a peasant largely depended on "heaven," that is, natural forces. But as a city girl from a cadre's family, economic security was not a top priority for me. What I found unappealing about a military-run state farm were the tight rules imposed upon their workers. I had never liked strict discipline and I knew I wouldn't make a good soldier. On the other hand, rural life was probably freer. So I signed up to go to Shanxi when the people from that province came to Beijing to recruit students. The nice thing about going to a village was that there was no political screening. Anybody could be a peasant.

Our county, Shanyin, was in a generally impoverished region. You talked about how much the scenery in Yunnan delighted you. I had a very different reaction to the northern Shanxi landscape. We left Beijing in late December so I didn't expect to see any green vegetation, but as the train was approaching our county, I was struck by how few trees there were on the horizon. Under the dim winter sun everything looked grey. I noticed stretches of white stuff covering the ground. Later I learned it was saline land. It didn't take an experienced eye to tell that this was a dismal growing region.

There must have been hundreds of Beijing youth sent to Shanyin, and we came primarily from two top secondary schools before the Cultural Revolution. Soon we were assigned to different villages. Our village was about 30 *li* from the county town. Several of us had brought bicycles from Beijing, so we rode the bikes to the village. The bicycles were not made for the bumpy country road. Within months they all fell apart. It showed how ignorant we were about rural conditions.

There were about 30 *zhiqing* in my village. My brother was one of several younger siblings included in my group. The students in his school went to a southern county in the same province, but my parents insisted that he join me to the north so that we could look after each other. This was the most parents could do under the circumstances, and it was also one nice thing about going to a village as opposed to a state farm. I know you could not bring siblings along to a state farm.

The villagers were pretty welcoming to us, at least not hostile. In regions where there was a scarcity of arable land the locals tended not to welcome outsiders—since more people meant more mouths to feed. In northern Shanxi there was a lot of land, lean but plentiful, so the villagers didn't mind having a few more hands. We were supposed to receive reeducation from the peasants, but most of them didn't seem to even know that was expected of them by Chairman Mao. In the end, however, the rural experience was profoundly educational for me, though probably not in the way intended by Mao.

The name of our village was Shanghexi. It had over 300 households, pretty big by local standards. At first we stayed separately with different peasant families. After a year or so we moved into a permanent ten-room house, built with the settlement money provided to us by the government, and lived together as one *zhiqing hu* (知青户 / educated youth household). The village made up a brigade in the commune system and was further divided into nine production teams. We *zhiqing* were assigned to work in different teams, each handling its own accounting. We earned work points instead of a monthly salary. An able-bodied male laborer earned 10 points a day; a teenage boy earned 8 points; I earned 7.5 points. After a year or so I was as good as a "full laborer," but I continued to earn less. The worth of a work point was determined by that year's harvest. At the end of an agricultural year, after deducting costs of grain and vegetables, which we had already received, we were paid the balance in cash. I never made more than 40 *yuan* in any given year. Part of the idea of coming to the countryside was to be self-supporting, but how could we achieve this goal with so little money? Most of us still needed financial help from family.

But we indeed enjoyed much more freedom in the village. Considering the ongoing political turmoil in many parts of the country, we were lucky to come to a relatively peaceful region. I couldn't tell how the Cultural Revolution had affected our village before we came, but by the time we got there the political movement had obviously run out of steam. Farm work was different from factory work. If peasants missed the spring planting season, the whole year would be wasted and the country would starve.

Politics Had a Different Flavor

Even though I'd been to the countryside before, I'd never had much contact with peasants and knew little about rural life. The first thing I noticed was how different the political and social atmosphere was in the village from the city. I was surprised to find that tradition still carried weight, while in urban

China it had been severely attacked and greatly weakened. Two-thirds of the villagers belonged to the "Liü" clan and the Liü people related to each other in accordance with a generational order. The higher a man's *beifen* (辈份 / generation), the more respect he would get. The head of the brigade was a person who had the highest *beifen* in the village and was therefore addressed respectfully as *laohan* (老汉 / old man) even though he was barely 40.

MA: But even in rural areas the new political culture must have some impact. No place could completely escape from it.

YE: You're right, but politics had a different flavor. Take the village meetings as an example. When there was a meeting—which was rare and often held in the evening—it was usually because the Party Central Committee had an instruction that needed to be passed onto the "masses." The meeting was often chaired by the village head. He didn't have much schooling, but he liked to imitate the bureaucratic tone and to show off his mastery of official jargon. The result was almost comical. While we *zhiqing* were trying hard not to laugh out loud, few villagers were paying much attention: men were dozing off, women were busy chatting, and children were running around.

I also remember a very different kind of meeting, which was extremely ugly and brutal. That day all of us—villagers and *zhiqing*—were required to go to a meeting held at the site of the commune headquarters. There we witnessed public executions. Among the people being shot were a young man and a middle-aged woman from my village, who were accused of killing the woman's husband by poison. The other death sentences also involved nonpolitical crimes. I was totally shocked by not just the execution scene, but also by what a few peasants did to the corpses: they gathered brains from the bullet-damaged heads. Among them I spotted a man from my team. I later learned that there was this local belief that brains could cure certain diseases such as serious skin ulcers. This folk custom reminded me of Lu Xun's story "Medicine," in which a character believed that blood from a newly executed person could cure his son's illness and soaked buns with the blood for his son to eat.[7]

I was haunted by what I saw for days to come. As I think about it now, I realize that public executions had a long history in China. As for using a dead person's brains for medicine, it was easier to regard such a custom as barbaric and ignorant, but it also showed the desperate needs of the peasants for adequate medical care. I knew that the man from my team was bothered constantly by ulcers. The two barefoot doctors[8] in my village were only able to provide basic treatments for simple problems. Apparently they had not been able to help him.

After the executions, many people in my village expressed sympathy for the dead young man. They thought the death sentence was too harsh for him.[9] According to them, the man was a good laborer and a decent guy. The woman, on the other hand, had long been known for her seductive behavior. It was she who had corrupted the man. The sad thing about the young man was that he was too poor to get a wife. So he became an easy prey for the woman. The opinions of the villagers certainly showed the usual gender bias, but they also highlighted the role played by poverty in this case.

Earlier you mentioned the Lin Biao Incident. It was extremely consequential for the development of the Cultural Revolution, but what did it mean to the villagers? After hearing the Party Central Committee's document on the subject, some villagers commented, "Lin Biao and Ye Qun (Lin's wife) were both on the state pay roll. Why did they still oppose Chairman Mao?" In the eyes of the peasants, who worked hard all year round but hardly saw any cash in the end, those who were paid a regular salary lived a good life. It was enviable enough to have just one person in a household earning an income. If both husband and wife held paying jobs, it would be heaven. Why weren't Lin Biao and Ye Qun satisfied? If I hadn't lived in the countryside for some time by then I would have found the villagers' remarks absurd and laughable. But I understood what they meant. The political struggle at the top failed to make much sense to the people at the bottom.

Sometimes I heard villagers say things such as grousing about the commune system that would definitely have been considered politically inappropriate in the city and could very well have gotten the people in trouble and even in prison. Weren't they afraid? The villagers told me they didn't care. As peasants they were stuck at the bottom of the society so they had nothing to lose. They were freer politically than city dwellers.

Of course the villagers who dared say outrageous things all came from politically safe families. Those from black categories had to be careful. There were three brothers in my team whose father was a former rich peasant. I never heard them say anything improper. We got along particularly well with Guisan, the middle brother. He was tall, handsome, and very skilled in farm work. He taught us how to plow and sometimes simply let us rest while he did the work. Guisan was almost 30 years old but still single. No family wanted to marry their daughter to a rich peasant's son even though villagers agreed in private that Guisan would make a good husband. For people like Guisan the shadow of class struggle weighed heavily. The *zhiqing* in my village were more or less fed up with class struggle rhetoric, so we were not afraid of being friendly with Guisan.

As city people we tended to think that we were smarter than country folks. Over time this perception was challenged. Once I went with some people to water a vegetable garden. I was standing in a low place when the water suddenly came down. Seeing my shoes were about to get wet, a peasant man told me to jump to a dry place and then remarked, "Whatever you do, always make sure you stand on dry ground." This was wisdom derived from a real-life situation and it would help me on several occasions later in my life. In the local community there were a few village scholars. Once one of them, an old man on my team, asked me what *ren* (humanity) meant in Confucian thinking. Knowing little about Confucianism, I was sweating all over. I was impressed by how intelligent his question was. It also surprised me that in this remote village you could find an interest in Confucianism whereas in urban China Confucius represented quintessential four-olds and nobody dared discuss his ideas.

On the other hand, we also came to see "poor and lower-middle peasants" in a more realistic way. By the class classification of the day they represented the politically most advanced people in rural China. They were glorified with all kinds of fine qualities in books we'd read and movies we'd seen. When an old man from the poor peasant category was assigned to cook for us, several girls commented how his face typified a poor peasant: dignified, honest, and so forth, as if a poor peasant should have a particular look or appearance. Soon, however, we found that our broomcorn millet reserve was rapidly decreasing. When it was clear that the old man had stolen it, those same girls got especially upset. He had taken the grain for the sake of his son whose wedding was about to take place. Broomcorn millet flour was the best material to make fried cakes, a local delicacy served on special occasions, yet each household only received a small amount every year. Stealing was fairly common among the villagers. Perhaps there was a reason.

I Now Knew the Face of Poverty

When we first arrived in the village we could hardly understand the northern Shanxi accent. To make communication easier with the local people we all learned to speak with their strong twang. Some *zhiqing* mastered it quickly. I felt inadequate that I couldn't do it as well. In the local vocabulary working in the field was called *shouku* (受苦 / enduring hardship or bitterness) and a good laborer was *hao shoukuren* (好受苦人 / a person good at enduring hardship or bitterness). The terms reflected the way of our farming: it was back-breaking manual labor. It probably had existed for thousands of years without much change. So working in the field was something to be endured, not enjoyed. Most of us *zhiqing* learned to be *hao shoukuren*. Once my team worked alongside another team. After watching me work for some time an old peasant in the other team remarked, "Now you know how to *shouku*." He was widely respected for his knowledge and skill in farming. I regard his comment as the highest praise I received in my five years' stay in the countryside.

Eventually I made a few village friends. They were either *laohan* (old men) or *xiao housheng* (小后生 / teenage boys). Women in my village seldom worked in the field so it was hard to get to know them well. I was particularly close to a *laohan* whose name was Liü Gaodian. He suffered from a constant stomachache and could only do light farm work. Because of this his work points were low. His oldest son had already started working in the field even though he was barely 14, and there were still three younger children in the household. So his family was particularly poor. Gaodian's wife was a kind-hearted woman from southern Shanxi. She was looked upon by the villagers as an outsider even though she had settled there for almost 20 years. Whenever there was a special occasion or a holiday, and there were many holidays on the lunar calendar that the peasants observed, I would be invited to a meal with the family. So the family was sort of my host family in the village. Their food was simple and even coarse by urban standards, but it showed the kindness of a peasant family. Almost all of us Beijing *zhiqing* had a host family or two in the village.

It was unsettling to see the poverty surrounding us. There were three scenes I will never forget. One occurred in a late fall. By then I had lived in the village for a number of years. Our team harvested potatoes earlier that day. In the evening we were going to divide up the potatoes so that each household would get its share—we received all our grains and vegetables this way. After supper I took a wicker basket to collect my share. When I came out of our alleyway, I saw a scene that has been forever frozen in my mind. Under the yellow streetlight, people from my team stood by a pile of potatoes. They were shivering in the cold wind in their shabby clothes. How they resembled a group sculpture of beggars! It was as though I was seeing my fellow team members for the first time. I now knew the face of poverty.

Once I was late for work in the field. By the time I got there the people had already disappeared in the thick and tall corn crops. Their shoes scattered outside the field—the villagers usually worked in barefoot during summer time to save shoes. I was alone with the shoes so I started to look at them: they were all homemade, many threadbare, and some completely broken. Years later I saw Van Gogh's painting of a broken shoe and I immediately made the connection. My life in the village taught me to tell a person's material situation by the conditions of his or her shoes.

There was another scene that has also stayed with me. One day I was visiting a peasant woman in her home. While I was sitting on the *kang* (brick bed) chatting with her, her little girl kept walking back and forth to the window behind us. I became curious and turned to see what was going on there. The girl was licking a candy, the cheapest kind sold in the village general store. She was clearly relishing every lick and there was a concentrated expression on her face. After a few light licks she carefully put the candy back on the edge of the window and walked away. After a few minutes she would go back and lick the candy again.

MA: What's so unusual about that?

YE: Rather than finishing the candy in a few bites, like I always did as a child, this little girl of no more than three years old already knew how to prolong a rare pleasure in her life. I was impressed by her incredible ability to restrain herself at this tender age. It was these details of everyday poverty that struck me the hardest.

In the first year I was in the village, each person on my team received ten kilos of wheat grain. By the time I left, an individual portion was reduced to 3.5 kilos. Only on special occasions such as a wedding ceremony or a big Chinese festival could a peasant family afford to have steamed wheat bread and some meat on their dinner table. The rest of the year their diet consisted mostly of corn bread, potatoes, and salted vegetables. In springtime when their grain reserve became low they even ate bread mixed with corn flour and edible wild herbs. Several months before the moon festival,[10] the villagers on my team had already started talking about what food to have for the holiday. Before coming to the countryside I was puzzled as to why we Chinese greeted each other by asking "have you eaten?" Now I understood it was only natural. Nothing was more important than food.

When we first arrived in the village, I thought there was little hope that we would ever return to the city. So I paid attention to the lifestyle of peasant women, trying to envision myself living a life like theirs. That prospect scared me. There was a young village woman my age who got married the year I came to the village. Three years later she was a mother of two and pregnant with the third. She looked tired all the time and her clothes were messy. Your description of the young Lisu woman in Yunnan reminded me of her. Peasant women were like reproductive machines. In our region unmarried young women were called *nüer* (女儿 / daughter), married women *nüren* (女人 / women). When a woman's reproductive years were over, say at age 45, she would be called *laoren* (老人), which simply meant "old person."

The practice of bride price still prevailed in our region. To get a wife, the groom's family had to pay the bride's family a substantial amount of money. A girl with good looks from a politically solid family would cost more than those without these credentials. The cost of bride price increased over the years I lived in the village from an average of 600 *yuan* to 1000 *yuan*. This reflected only cash payment and didn't include other bride expenses such as new sets of clothes, a watch, or a bicycle.

When we *zhiqing* first learned of this custom, we were appalled. Wasn't this in essence marriage for sale? We thought such things had disappeared with the founding of the PRC. We were further surprised when the women we talked to all defended the practice. We had assumed that they would feel insulted because the custom treated them as commodities. Instead they told us it was only fair to compensate the parents for raising a daughter: after marriage the girl would become a member of another family and was no longer able to help her natal family. Furthermore, for many girls this was the only time they got to wear nice clothes. Some used this opportunity to show off their new outfits by walking back and forth along the dirt village road. I was amused, but I also felt sad for them.

Marriages were made through matchmakers or family friends. Before marriage the young man and woman would meet a few times but there would always be other people present. I tried to picture myself leaving the natal community to go to a village miles away to marry a strange man, and I felt completely chilled. There had been a number of love affairs among the young people in my village and the locals talked about their affairs with sympathy, but none of the lovers ended up marrying each other.

To minimize cash flow, a family with a son and a daughter would seek another family with a son and a daughter of comparable age to make a double-marriage deal. This was how poor people married their children. Since the primary concern was to save money, the four young people involved had even less say in their marriages. Over the years I was in the village exchange marriage became increasingly common.

A young man from my team had such a marriage. His family lived next door to us so he often visited our *zhiqing* yard. Curious about the outside world, he came to listen to the radio, read newspapers and books, and chat with the boys. He liked to show that he knew everything, so he got the nickname "*laodong*," meaning "know-it-all." He was very smart and fairly good-looking. His family had no money so his parents opted for exchange marriages for *Laodong* and his younger sister. After the decision was made, *Laodong* became visibly quiet. We all knew he was unhappy. He had a lover in the village, a pretty girl, but she would be too costly for his family. After his marriage he spent even more time in our yard, a sign that he was not very fond of his wife. We felt sorry for *Laodong*. But if you think about it, his sister's situation was even more pathetic. She was only 16, yet she had to get married so that her elder brother, who was then about 25, could get a wife. Exchange marriages were unfair to both men and women, but women often fared even worse in the bargain.

I was the only female laborer on my team regularly working in the field. Only occasionally would some unmarried young women join us. The men cracked dirty jokes all the time during work. At first I felt very uncomfortable. Later I realized they would do it with or without my presence. Sex jokes made monotonous labor more bearable and their main audience was *xiao housheng* (young adults). You might even say that these jokes served as sex education for the teenage boys, who were a lot more knowledgeable about sex than city youth my age.

Still I felt safe working among peasant men. When we first arrived some villagers privately inquired whether any of us would consider taking a local husband, assuming a city girl would not fetch a big bride price. Once they realized that we were not interested, they left us alone.

I noticed one interesting phenomenon after living in the village for some time. It seemed that the male peasants didn't quite view us female *zhiqing* as women. I overheard them remark more than once that the urban girls were "not like women." I thought it was possibly because we were doing man's work. By laboring in the field rather than taking care of household chores at home, we *zhiqing* girls clearly broke local gender norms. Something subtler may also have been going on here. We had acquired a tendency to talk and laugh loudly, which male peasants probably considered unfeminine.

There was more sexual freedom in rural areas. From time to time we heard of extramarital affairs. The people involved were not stigmatized as they would be in cities. Occasionally I saw young men and woman openly necking. I was shocked, but the villagers laughed heartily. Everybody had a good time.

An Invisible Wall

MA: What you said gives me the impression that you *zhiqing* got along very well with the villagers. This makes me envious. On the state farm we had little contact with the local people.

YE: I guess as individuals we did all right. But as a group, I have to say that our relationship with the local people was rather superficial. A major frustration I felt in those years was my inability to break through the invisible wall separating us from the peasants. I had come to the countryside somewhat reluctantly, but after I saw what life was like for the peasants I had the urge to do something to help. In other villages in my county some Beijing *zhiqing* were contributing to local life by serving as accountants, teachers, barefoot doctors, and even team and brigade leaders. They were using their knowledge to improve rural conditions. I admired them very much. At one point I was strongly tempted to transfer to a village where Beijing *zhiqing* were more actively involved in local affairs. But in the end it was only a thought. Whenever I thought about those *zhiqing* who were doing something for their community, I would break out in a sweat.

I guess how well *zhiqing* integrated into local life depended a lot on the composition of the *zhiqing* group and the leadership of the group. The *zhiqing* in my village might work hard in the field and even get along well with individual villagers, but their hearts lay elsewhere. Physically we lived in the village, but intellectually and emotionally we were apart from the village. I felt awful about our rather insulated life in the midst of an impoverished rural community. How I wished there were people among us who wanted to do something to help the village. I would definitely follow the lead. By myself I didn't know how to start and what to do. It was difficult for a young urban woman to do much on her own. But of course this was an excuse.

Soon after we arrived in the village, the *zhiqing* divided into two factions. It had nothing to do with family background. Most of the *zhiqing* in my village were cadres' children. It's worth adding here that coming to the countryside had a leveling impact on us. There was no more clear-cut division between the cadres' children and a few people among us who were not from this family background. The importance of "birth" had diminished, since we were all in the same boat as *zhiqing*. Almost everybody aligned with one faction or the other. Boys took the lead and girls followed suit. There was nothing worth mentioning about the reasons for the split. I think the divide resulted more from an appetite for power on the part of some boys who probably had acquired a taste for it earlier in the Cultural Revolution. I found the whole thing silly and stayed away from both factions.

The most important activity for a faction was *dapinghuo*, meaning "sharing food." What we had everyday at the *zhiqing* canteen was corn bread, millet porridge, and preserved cabbages and carrots. At first food was rationed because there wasn't enough of it. There were even times when some boys waited outside the *zhiqing* canteen to ask for leftover corn bread from the girls. Later grain was no longer a problem, but there were hardly any fresh vegetables, let alone meat. Because of this poor diet, every time we went back to Beijing for a visit we would bring back foodstuffs such as sausages and dried noodles. During *dapinghuo* people from the same faction would pool their food together and enjoy a nice meal. At times like this I would find myself having no place to go. I spent the first moon festival in the countryside by myself while my roommate went to her faction's party. Looking up at the full moon in a clear sky I felt intensely alone. I was a double outsider both in the *zhiqing* group and the village community.

Soon I was shocked to learn that some *zhiqing* in my village were involved in premarital sex. My team's stable was only separated from our *zhiqing* yard by a low wall. One day a used condom was found on the stable ground and the villagers believed that it must have been thrown over from the other side. By now I had accepted a more relaxed attitude toward sex among the peasants, but when it was done by people among *us*, I was stunned. It was so wrong. The whole thing was so disturbing to me that I felt the sky had suddenly darkened. This feeling lasted for a couple of days. No political event had ever provoked such a strong reaction in me. I'm still puzzled by why I reacted this way.

MA: As for me, I find it amazing that some *zhiqing* in your village were not only daring enough to engage in sex but also sophisticated enough to use condoms. I can't imagine this happening on my farm.

YE: As a matter of fact, there were a lot of romances going on among the *zhiqing*, and I was always the last to know. Someone once joked that a "red thread of love" was running through the entire period we were in the village. What else would you expect from a bunch of young men and women free from parents' watchful eye and in a sexually casual environment?

"Singing Our Turbulent Youth"

YE: As time went by some *zhiqing* began to leave the village, either to join the military or to work in a city factory. This always meant that their parents' problems were cleared. I eventually realized that some day I might also be able to go. As the number of *zhiqing* shrank, factional divide also faded. I became more drawn to the *zhiqing* circle, even though at the back of my mind lingered a regret that I had failed to break the invisible wall separating us from the peasants. There would be more sexual liaisons among the *zhiqing*, but I stopped being surprised. I was conservative in my personal conduct, but my puritanical thinking dissolved into a more tolerant attitude toward other people's "loose" behavior.

I came to appreciate the liberal spirit of my *zhiqing* group. It was not only reflected in people's personal conduct but more in their political attitude. There was an underlying resentment against the Cultural Revolution. Several people's fathers were in prison and their children didn't even know where they were being held. One guy's father committed suicide and the son heard the news in the village. The group was largely made up of children of the politically dispossessed elite due to the Cultural Revolution. In many ways I belonged to this group, even though I had reservations about it. Our political fate was closely linked to that of the country. A change in the political climate could improve or worsen our own personal lot. The Lin Biao Incident took us by surprise, but it didn't shake us the way it did many other people. We received the news with great joy and hoped that the country would subsequently turn away from the radical leftist path. Some people became emboldened after the incident and began to openly criticize Jiang Qing and the other Cultural Revolution leaders. They knew they were safe among this *zhiqing* group. I found myself breathing more easily in this environment and almost forgot about my fears.

Another nice thing about our *zhiqing* group was that many of us shared a common interest in learning. One guy brought two huge trunks of his father's books to the village. The father, once a prominent journalist and later a high ranking official, had a marvelous collection of classical Chinese and European literature. Before he went to a "cadres' school"[11] in another province he divided the books among his children and we all became the beneficiaries. Occasionally we also borrowed books from *zhiqing* in neighboring villages. Once I had to finish Standahl's *The Red and the Black* in one night before passing it to the next person in line. I stayed up the whole night reading the book.

One memorable experience we had was hearing the entire story of *The Count of Monte Cristo* told by a boy who had recently read the book. For a week or so we gathered in his room every evening after supper, sitting around him on campstools made of straw. Since nobody else had read the novel we couldn't tell if he was faithful to the original tale. But even if he wasn't nobody would care, we simply enjoyed the story telling. One evening I was late for the event. Peeping through the window I saw people sitting in a circle listening to the boy attentively. There was something touching about the scene.

With or without books, people continued their pursuit of knowledge. One boy was a physics nut. He often adjusted the angle of his hoe at the end of the day, applying his knowledge of mechanics to make his hoe more labor efficient. Another boy was interested in international affairs. His hobby was to gather every piece of information he could find about a foreign country: climate, geography, population, and so on. The data primarily came from *The People's Daily*—the only paper available to us. His newspaper clippings eventually filled several thick volumes of used magazines. He liked to challenge us to test him about any country in the world, the more obscure the better.

There was no electricity when we first arrived in the village. In the third year the area was connected to a power plant. By then we had become accustomed to physical labor and we needed release for our surplus energy, especially during the long winter months when there was little work in the field. Some of us began to make systematic study plans. My brother finished studying senior high math and physics on his own. Nobody knew if colleges would ever be open again, but the desire for learning was too strong for us to care about its practical value. Several people decided to study English and it was fun to join them. Many of us had short-wave radios. It was amazing how easily we could receive foreign broadcasts such as VOA (Voice of America), BBC, and Radio Moscow in this remote region.

MA: You could have been arrested for listening to "enemy broadcasts!"

YE: We were careful. But I don't think the village leaders would bother us even if they found out. VOA had a program called "Special English," which contained limited vocabulary and the pace of speech was very slow, so I could follow. For a while the topic was American founding fathers. I was intrigued by Thomas Jefferson's ideas about individual rights and civil liberty. Imagine Jefferson appealing to a young Chinese in a poor rural village.

Music was a big part of our lives. Two boys brought musical instruments: an accordion and a violin. Melodies often floated from our *zhiqing* yard. We sang Chinese songs from the 1950s and 1960s, Russian songs, and folk songs from the rest of the world. Somebody had a copy of *Two Hundred Foreign Folk Songs*, which contained pieces like "Oh Susanna" and "Return to Sorrento." These songs had been criticized earlier in the Cultural Revolution, but now they became very popular among us. Our favorite was a Russian song from World War II called "Singing Our Turbulent Youth" (歌唱动荡的青春). It was about love, friendship, and youthful yearnings to accomplish great deeds in the midst of war. The title immediately resonated with us. We liked it so much that we claimed it as our "village song."

Singing songs helped us reconnect to feelings that had been long condemned and repressed. We liked love songs the best. I still remember one moonlit night filled with such songs. Our *zhiqing* yard was located at the edge of the village. That evening people from one faction were singing in the yard. They covered almost all the love songs from *Two Hundred Foreign Folk Songs*, singing one after another, not aware how late it was getting. There was still a factional division at the time, but nobody complained that it was too late. The rest of us stayed up inside enjoying their singing. It was truly a moonlight concert.

MA: I'm impressed by how rich your life was. The things you guys did in the village would be unthinkable for us on the farm.

YE: Your life was more regulated. We were left with space to create our own. This was the nice thing about coming to the countryside. But if you think about it, it was odd that an urban youth culture would flourish in the midst of rural poverty.

But what we did also could be viewed as an escape from the dreariness of our everyday existence. Reading nineteenth-century Russian novels, listening to VOA, and singing Latin American love songs all expressed a yearning for things beyond our reach. There was a mountain to the south of our village known for its beautiful scenery. One sunny autumn day several of us decided to check it out. It was a long walk from our village but our spirits were high. One boy, the "foreign affairs expert," remarked, "Let's pretend we are a tour group from Australia." We all laughed. "Tour" and "Australia" sounded so remote from our reality.

The villagers, especially the *xiao housheng* (young adults), also had their fantasies. Imagining life in the city was their tireless pastime. When we were working in the field they often asked us what city life was like. In their minds city dwellers had a lot of leisure. Much of their time was spent on watching films in grand theatres and walking on paved streets—men and women holding hands. Older peasants seldom joined our conversation. They probably had stopped dreaming a long time ago.

My five years in the village allowed me to observe the relationship between peasants and local cadres. Most of the cadres at the brigade level did not take part in agricultural work in the field, yet they all earned full work points. The peasants complained about it all the time behind the cadres' backs. It was not uncommon for people in a leadership position to abuse power. Our relationship with our team leader was particularly tense. He was quite tall, so we called him "*qichihui*" (七尺灰 / "bad tall guy") behind his back. *Qichihui* seldom came to work in the field. He claimed that he needed to inspect crops in various fields. The peasants described his job as "strolling." Without breaking a sweat, he earned ten full work points a day.

When *qichihui* was not with us, we received orders from the deputy team leader. His style was rather lenient. After we got to the field, he would say, "Let's smoke a pipe." We would sit down on the ground and some people would smoke one or two or three pipes. Then the deputy leader would slowly get up, signaling "time to work." In the middle of the day we would take a break. This was how peasants worked. Some teenage boys loafed on the job by hoeing only the beginning of a crop row, skipping much of the middle part, and then rushing to the end. The older peasants showed a better work ethic, but they didn't seem to be bothered by the youngsters' shoddy performance. At first I was disturbed. How could the kids cheat *jiti* (集体 / the collective) like this? It didn't take me long to realize that most of the peasants didn't really care about *jiti*.

When *qichihui* showed up, nobody dared to cheat or to be lazy. The guy was in the prime of his life and was full of energy. He often came in the middle of the morning after we had been working for several hours. He had long legs and moved with big steps, and we had to follow his fast pace. When it was close to noontime, I could hear my stomach growl. We *zhiqing* at least had had corn bread for breakfast, but most of the villagers had eaten only thin porridge, at best with one or two slices of potato in it. They must have felt even hungrier. Other teams passed our field on their way back to the village for lunch. *Qichihui* acted as if he didn't notice them. The sun was burning and the crop row seemed unbearably long.

In moments like this I would curse *qichihui* in my heart, saying "you can't treat us like this!" These words were on the tip of my tongue but they never came out. We suffered this kind of mistreatment periodically, and we never knew when it would befall us. There was so much resentment against *qichihui* among the team members that behind his back people used the worst language to curse him. But when he was around nobody dared to confront him. His *beifen* (generational rank) was very high and he must have powerful people backing him up at the brigade level. I thought I should protest on behalf of my fellow team members. But in the end I said nothing. I felt intensely guilty about my cowardliness.

MA: Did you always work in the field?

YE: Most of the time. Once for several months I worked as an accountant for the brigade flourmill. The brigade leaders decided to offer the job to *zhiqing* to avoid embezzlement, which had been a common problem with previous accountants. My job was to run the machines and to keep the books. At the end of the day I was covered with flour, looking like a white-haired girl. One thing I learned from this job was how *zou houmen* (走后门 / going through the backdoor) worked. Even cadres working in the commune headquarters eight *li* away would bring grain to the mill and expect free service. My assistant, a local person, understood their intension. He would grind the grain and put their bags in a safe corner for them to pick up. Meanwhile some of my villager friends didn't want to pay either. They nodded at me and left their grain bags behind.

Eventually I learned to assess each situation. I couldn't make the cadres pay, so I had to accept that reality. But the rest of the people had to pay or I would be running a losing business. Where to draw the line? I had to let my friends know that they needed to pay. The only exception was Gaodian. He earned fewer work points because of his poor health, yet he had to support a large family. I let his family go without paying. When I counted the earnings at the end of the day, I often felt bewildered. I was not able to help most of the needy people, while at the same time I was perpetuating cadres' privilege. Besides who knew what would happen to the money once it entered the brigade coffer. I quit the job after a few months and went back to work in the field. I had always wanted to do something worthwhile in the village other than just being a farm hand. But the experience at the flourmill left me in a state of disillusionment.

The first several years I worked in the field, farming gave me joy. I was proud that the seeds I planted in the spring grew into crops by fall. Holding the harvest in my arms was gratifying. But this romantic feeling eventually faded. After years of repetitive physical labor I felt my life was stagnant.

In August 1973, I left the village to attend college in Beijing. To the south of our village stood two mountains that I saw everyday from my window, one was called *mantou shan* (馒头山 / the mountain of steamed bun), the other "*caoduo shan*" (草垛山 / the mountain of haystacks). The names captured the shapes of the mountaintops. They also expressed the peasants' simple wish that there be plenty of steamed buns for people and a sufficient supply of hay for draft animals. Riding a horse-drawn cart to the county site to take the train, I turned my face to the south and said good-bye to the mountains in my heart. Once again I was overcome by a strong feeling of guilt. I had done little to help the local people.

By the time I left, the majority of the *zhiqing* in my village had already gone, including my brother. Our yard looked like a wasteland. Where there used to be a vegetable garden and pigsty, now the grass was knee high and the pigsty long gone. Most of the ten rooms were vacant and much of the music and laughter had disappeared.

I left the village with many questions on my mind: why did our hard labor produce so meager a reward? Why did the peasants have little incentive to work hard? Why was there so much tension between the peasants and the cadres? Somehow I sensed that the commune system had failed to fulfill its promise, but I didn't think hard and deep about why it was so. Around this time there were some Beijing zhiqing who gathered together to discuss similar questions. Among them were some original Red Guards. To seek answers they read all kinds of theoretical works, Marxist or not. They represented the more serious side of a youth culture that flourished in some zhiqing communities across the country. When the reform era began in the late 1970s some of these people would play a vanguard role, pushing for economic and political changes in both rural and urban China. I admired them very much. The zhiqing in my village were not of this type.

I was 18 when I first arrived in the countryside. By the time I left I was 23. The prime years of my youth were spent in Shanghexi, a poor village in northern Shanxi. During the five years I was there, I had a taste of what life was like for peasants, who composed the vast majority of China's population. If asked for one word to describe that life, I would choose "kunan" (苦难 / tribulation). I had a taste of it, though for me it was neither deep nor long. Whenever I read something related to this theme, a chord is struck inside me. I am constantly reminded of who I am and where I came from. Wherever I go in the world, be it Beijing or Boston, there always will be a village in China I regard as mine. The five years there grounded me in China and in life.

Yet in the end I had to leave. I didn't want to spend the rest of my life as a peasant. At the time of my departure I didn't ask why I could go while the peasants were stuck in the soil. I didn't question the fundamental inequality between urban and rural populations. Two years before I left the countryside I had joined a work team and spent a winter inspecting another village's financial condition. There I made a male friend, a gentle and intelligent young man. He was a teacher in the village school and a peasant son. We enjoyed each other's company, but we also knew that our feelings toward each other wouldn't lead anywhere. We didn't belong to the same world.

*   *   *

In September 1973 both Ma Xiaodong and I went back to Beijing for college. There is a story about the way I finally got to college. The previous year I was recommended by the peasants in my village to go to the prestigious Beijing University, only to learn in the last minute that I didn't meet with political approval and so couldn't go. Later I found that I was rejected because of my old diary, the one seized during a search of our home early in the Cultural Revolution. Labeled as "counterrevolutionary," it was placed in my dossier and followed me all the way to Shanxi without my awareness.

Due to a more liberal political climate around 1972, I was able to get the diary removed from my dossier. This enabled me to go to college the following year. When the diary was finally returned to me, I found dirty fingerprints and red pencil markings throughout the pages. It was clear the diary had passed through many strangers' hands. Written during my teen years, the diary contained my doubts about the Cultural Revolution along with my misty sexual yearnings. I felt terribly violated.

FIVE

Worker–Peasant–Soldier Students

Colleges reopened their doors in the early 1970s after stopping admissions in 1966. In the fall of 1973 both Ma Xiaodong and I went back to Beijing to attend college. We felt luckier than most of our peers who didn't have the opportunity to resume formal education. We went to college via recommendations instead of taking an entrance examination. Once in college we were bestowed a glorifying title: "worker–peasant–soldier students." This title reflected the composition of the student body. Rather than recruiting current high school graduates, colleges now only admitted people with practical experience.[1] After five years of country life, we earned the qualification of "peasant" (me) and "farm worker" (Ma) respectively. The new recruitment policy reflected the Cultural Revolution leaders' decision to reform higher education, which was considered a stronghold of bourgeois revisionist thinking. In reality, however, this policy was inherently arbitrary and prone to abuse. Moreover the emphasis on political rather than academic criteria resulted in a great disparity in the levels of preparation among the students and made teaching very challenging. It also created tension in the student body.

Our college years (1973–1976) coincided with the last years of the Cultural Revolution. During those years a fierce struggle ensued between moderate leaders such as Zhou Enlai and Deng Xiaoping and ultra-leftist Cultural Revolution leaders represented by Mao's wife Jiang Qing. Moderates were trying to reestablish normalcy in areas such as economy and education. Ultra-leftists, on the other hand, were determined to continue the radical path. College campuses became a political battlefield between the two factions, where the ultra-leftists often had an upper hand. Academic studies were frequently interrupted by political campaigns launched by the radical faction. Moreover, to comply with Mao's idea that true knowledge could only be derived from real life, students constantly left the classroom to go to factories, villages, and military camps, a practice called "opening schools to society."

Ma Xiaodong and I went to the same school, Beijing Normal College. We didn't know each other at the time though, as we were affiliated with two different departments: Ma Xiaodong was in Chinese language and literature, and I was in foreign languages. As a local college, most students came from either one of the two backgrounds: people with peasant origin from rural areas surrounding Beijing and former zhiqing, like Ma and me, who had recently returned to their home city. Generally speaking the educational level of people in the latter group was higher.

This was a peculiar period in the history of Chinese higher education, when politics presided over academic learning and tension was embedded in the student body. For Ma Xiaodong and I this was a frustrating time. Ma fought hard to maintain her idealism and in the end decided to return to the countryside in order to be true to her ideals. I had a distressful time trying to survive a campus life that was politically oppressive and academically depressing. With hindsight, our three years of college life witnessed the last nasty gasp of ultra-left politics.

Ye Weili's Story: The Painted Skin

YE: Once back in the city, I immediately felt the oppressiveness of ultra-left politics. I realized right away that urban dwellers were first and foremost political beings. I missed the much freer atmosphere in the country. Beijing Normal College was like a political training camp rather than an institute for higher learning. On top of the endless political meetings, our daily life was strictly regimented: drills in the morning and a bell to signal lights out at night. You know I had never liked strict discipline. I resented the highly politicized and semi-military way in the college.

It didn't take long for me to sense that some people from rural origins didn't trust us urban students. There were many decent individuals in this rural group, but I must say I had problems with some student leaders, all of whom happened to come from peasant background. Because they were in a position of power, I felt I was under their watchful eye all the time. It made me very uncomfortable. After years of living in the countryside I came to see myself as half a peasant and felt an affinity for rural people. I was really puzzled by the leaders' distrust. I've thought a lot about the reasons. I now see that the tension reflected a deep gulf between urban and rural China.

I thought my years of country life had shortened my distance from the peasant class, but I was naïve. If previously it was the peasants who were looked down upon by city people, now what I experienced was a reverse discrimination by some people of peasant origin. This was a new experience for me.

An incident in my English class really turned me off. A student who was a returned *zhiqing* was rudely interrupted in the middle of answering the teacher's question by another student, who happened to be a party leader in our department. She told the man in a stern voice, "You have practiced enough." The whole class was stunned. After witnessing this encounter, I never voluntarily spoke in class again, even though oral exercises were essential for language learning. Let people from rural background have more opportunities.

Of course this was an extreme case, but it highlighted the great disparity in our levels of English. When we entered college, some of us were quite advanced. Others, like most of the students with rural origin, barely knew the alphabet. This mixed ability grouping made teaching extremely difficult. I often felt bored in class. In order not to totally waste time, I sometimes would bring a book and quietly read it by myself. My seat was at the back of the classroom so few people would notice. The teachers knew what I was doing but they never intervened.

But the real issue was not that I didn't get to practice in class. Our greatest problem was that we spent too little time in the classroom. A student in our department once tallied the days we had actually spent in class the previous school year: we were on campus only for about one-third of the time; the rest was spent on opening schools to society, mostly in the countryside. Our subject of study was English language, but systematic training was constantly interrupted.

Over time I learned to make use of any situation I found myself in to learn something . . . almost anything. During the campaign against Confucius,[2] we were allowed to read texts in classical Chinese in order to criticize Confucius. I was not at all interested in the campaign, but I used the opportunity to improve my classical Chinese. The campaign became a cover. Then we spent a month in an army camp. I became interested in target shooting. It was not that I had suddenly turned militant. I clung to anything technical to have a break from the nonsense of politics.

As part of opening schools to society, we spent nearly a full semester doing student teaching in secondary schools in the industrial western Beijing. Our academic training barely qualified us to teach, but students didn't want to learn anyhow. Vandalism was common in many schools and windowpanes were favorite targets for the students. I learned to identify a school by looking to see if the building still had full glass. If most of the windows were broken, it surely was a school. The first day I arrived in my class somebody broke the blackboard, leaving a hole about the size of a basin. The hole stayed there for the rest of the semester, reminding me how absurd the teaching environment was. Because most of them would be sent down to the countryside after graduation, my students had no incentive to study. They kept asking me, "What's the use of learning English?" I didn't know what to say. I spent more time dealing with student discipline problems than teaching any English. The prospect of working in such a school after graduation truly chilled me.

Even when we went back to campus, academic learning was not encouraged. It was only secondary to reformation of the old educational system. Students interested in academic studies, especially those from urban background, could easily be accused of pursuing selfish goals. I often had to hide in a quiet corner to do my studies. I hated this. Why couldn't we legitimately study? Weren't we in college?

What bothered me even more were the constant political meetings we had to attend. At those meetings each student had to state his or her position on issues. There had hardly been any meetings in the countryside so I didn't know how to make a public speech. The first political campaign we had after arriving at the college was to counter the alleged revival of a bourgeois educational line. Zhou Enlai and Deng Xiaoping's names were not mentioned but their policies were reproached, such as their effort to raise academic standards at colleges. When I first spoke at such a meeting, I blushed badly, not only because I was not used to public speaking but also because I had to say things I didn't believe. I was sympathetic to Zhou and Deng's policies, but I knew better than to say what was truly on my mind.

Eventually I was able to tell political lies without blushing. By then I had become rather cynical. All they wanted to hear were lies. Why not give them? At the same time, the image of the ghost in Pu Songling's famous story, "The Painted Skin,"[3] (画皮 / *huapi*) started haunting me. When the ghost went out he would wear a painted human skin in the shape of a beautiful woman. Once he retreated to his own place he would take off the painted skin. Then his true identity was revealed: a monstrous-looking ghost.

MA: What did the story have to do with you?

YE: I saw myself as that ghost. What I showed to the world was not the real me but somebody with a painted skin. I imagined that when I was by myself I would take off the skin, examine it, and perhaps even add a little more paint. I would say to myself, "Let me see how it looks," as if it were a piece of work I created—a fake me.

At the end of my college years, I felt I had learned more about political survival than anything else. But I paid a mental toll for it. During the last few months in college I began to feel dizzy and the symptom would attack me at anytime. The doctor said I was suffering from an autonomic nerve disorder. I knew I was simply too unhappy.

MA Xiaodong's Story: Looking for Ways to Keep Up My Spirits

MA: I was not as bothered by the regimented routine as you were, since I had lived a semi-military life on the state farm for many years. My spirits were high when I first arrived at our college campus. People came out to help me with my luggage, which reminded me of my first day in secondary school. How I wanted to be a good member in this new community!

Soon, however, I heard some classmates say that they thought I was "aloof, proud, and unapproachable." The implication was that I looked down upon people from rural background. I was disturbed by this criticism and asked a roommate how I had given others this impression. She told me, "It's your looks." I picked up a mirror and examined myself. How did I look different from others? I thought the whole thing was absurd. If it was my looks, there was nothing I could do.

I had a theory about the tension between some people from peasant background and us urban students: they generally didn't do as well academically as we, so they tried to compensate for their academic inadequacy by posturing as politically superior to us. In any event, I found life in college much more complicated than on the farm. I used to be able to prove myself with hard work and to say what was on my mind. Now things were different. After the first several weeks of classes I became dissatisfied with the quality of lectures given by some teachers. In one lecture the professor denounced all Western classical novels. I thought what he said was unconvincing so I expressed this opinion during a discussion session. Soon I was criticized by some people for being too "right-leaning." I had to watch my mouth from then on.

Realizing there was little I could learn from the teachers' lectures, I often used class time to rest. After class I would borrow books and read on my own. At first I was not very careful. Then I began to hear complaints about my spending too much time on academic studies. The implication was that I didn't pay sufficient attention to political studies. A friend advised me not to read books in public places. She said, "Look at me. I often do my reading in bed." She slept on the top bunk so nobody could see what she was reading up there.

But there weren't many books to borrow from the school library. Most literary classics were regarded as politically incorrect and were not available to even us Chinese literature majors. I had to read what I could get. So I read a lot of Lu Xun. But the problem was finding time to read Lu Xun. Classes were often cancelled for political activities. And like your department, we also often left the classroom to go to villages and factories. I didn't object to the idea of learning from society, but I felt that we could do that after graduation. The three years of college were precious and we should make good use of them. I was very unhappy about this situation.

I tried to be active politically and applied for membership in the Communist Party. I wanted to join the party because it had always been an honorable organization in my mind and a place for the most outstanding people. My department's party branch was considering my application. They kept testing me and raising new issues. I felt constantly being pushed into a corner. It was hard to gain the trust of the party leaders; most of them also came from peasant background as in your department. By the time I finally became a party member, I had lost much of the initial enthusiasm.

YE: In my department, none of the urban students were admitted into the party. The party branch earned the reputation as a peasant party. Joining the organization was out of the question for me. I would be very happy if the party people left me alone.

My experience of joining the party was not uplifting. I was looking for ways to keep up my spirits. A year or so before our graduation I heard that a former *zhiqing*, now a student at Beijing University, was planning to return to his old village in Heilongjiang province after graduation. His name was Wong. I could hardly believe that such people still existed. He was the kind of person I had always been looking for—someone with ideals. I went to meet him right away and decided to follow him to his village after graduation.

YE: Going back to the countryside again? Few people would even think about this option after finally returning to the city.

MA: My friends were all puzzled by my decision. My parents were very upset. I had longed for a more meaningful life and was turned off by the prospect of teaching in a secondary school in Beijing after graduation. I couldn't imagine myself following the tedious routine of classroom teaching. I needed something larger. Besides, I was aware of the horrible conditions in secondary schools at this time.

But to tell you the truth, I also harbored mixed feelings about leaving Beijing. One night I had a dream. In the dream I heard the whistle of a train and the train was going to nowhere but Yunnan. I woke up in a cold sweat.

At that moment I realized that deep inside I was scared of going back to Yunnan. This thought disturbed me deeply. How had I become like those people who were afraid of hardship?

Wong impressed me at first sight. He was tall, thin, very articulate, and full of enthusiasm. If he had been born in a different time he would have been a natural revolutionary leader. I fell in love with him right away. If not for him, I probably would not have gone to Heilongjiang.

When I arrived in the village a few months after the graduation, Wong was already there. He came right after his graduation and was now the head of the brigade. I worked under him as the accountant. The person who held the position previously, a local guy, had been found guilty of embezzlement. The villagers trusted that we *zhiqing* would be more honest.

As a leader, Wong was extremely hard working and had great personal integrity. His goal was to lift the peasants from poverty. He was the first to bear hardship and the last to enjoy comfort. Wong knew how to get people to follow his lead. He enjoyed a lot of respect from the villagers. You may even say that he had charisma.

After a while, however, I began to wonder about his approach to solving the problem of rural poverty. He was primarily running a one-man show. This was before economic reform in rural China. In the village everything depended on Wong's personal authority and charm. When he was around, things were fine. But when he was away, decisions had to be delayed and things would break down. Knowing that the village couldn't do without him, he worked at the expense of his own health. Later Wong suffered from a serious illness and had to go back to Beijing for treatment. After he was gone, the rest of us *zhiqing* realized that there was not much we could do. One after another we all left.

YE: What about your personal relationship with him?

MA: It didn't work out.

Still, I admire Wong's spirit. Looking back, I don't regret my time spent in Heilongjiang. Thanks to it, along with my experience in Yunnan, I became more aware of the poverty of peasants in rural China.

1976 was our last year in college and a remarkable year for China. It began with Premier Zhou Enlai's death in January and ended with Mao Zedong's death in September. Zhou's death was viewed by many Chinese as an enormous loss. The Cultural Revolution had exposed ordinary citizens to too much ugly politics. Zhou symbolized conscience and common sense in many people's hearts. In early April there was the qingming festival [4] *and a time in Chinese tradition to pay homage to the dead. People all over the country used this opportunity to mourn Zhou's death. In Beijing the gathering place was Tiananmen Square. The mourning there soon turned into an open political protest against ultra-leftist politics.*

I was at the square on the day of qingming. The gigantic square was a sea of people. The Monument of People's Heroes, which bore Zhou's calligraphy at the back, was buried by wreaths. Many people made speeches and read aloud poems to express their sorrow over Zhou's death and to critique, satire, and even directly attack Mao's wife Jiang Qing and other Cultural Revolution leaders. Some even bold enough to allude to Mao and compare him to Qinshi Huangdi, an emperor in Chinese history known for cruelty. Until then I was not sure how other people felt about the political situation in China. I only dared speak my mind with my family and a few trusted friends. At the square I realized I was not alone. Although we didn't know each other personally, I was among my own people. It was empowering. Among the people in the huge crowd there were many from my age cohort. Ten years earlier, in 1966, the same people shouted "Long live Chairman Mao"! infront of the balcony of Tiananmen. Now they gathered at the square for a very different purpose. It was only a short walk from the gate of Tiananmen to the Monument of People's Heroes, but as somebody from my generation remarked, "It has taken us ten years to cover the distance."

Soon, however, the qingming event was labeled as counter-reactionary by the ultra-leftist leaders backed by Mao. The following months saw a round of political persecution. Deng Xiaoping was accused of being the "black hand" behind the scene and was forced to step down. The political atmosphere turned oppressive again.

Mao died a few months later. I felt differently about his death. I was anxious, but not sad. Where would the country go now? Many people feared that Mao's death might mean a complete takeover by the ultra-leftists.

Within a month of Mao's death Jiang Qing and three other ultra-leftist leaders, known as the Gang of Four, were arrested. The whole country burst into joy. The Cultural Revolution had finally come to an end.

The Reform Era

In 1978 China entered a new era of reform and opening-up, and has since undergone profound transformation economically, socially, and culturally. The change in the political realm has been less impressive. The shift from the Cultural Revolution's obsession with continuous revolution under a proletarian dictatorship to social relaxation and economic development has been truly phenomenal. Meanwhile there is still a long way to go to realize a genuine political reform that was first openly called for during the Beijing Democracy Wall Movement in 1978–1979.

The 1980s was a dynamic decade for China. Forces both within and without the political establishment worked together to push for a more transparent and humane society despite persistent opposition from the conservatives. Change— small and big, subtle and obvious—began to be part of Chinese life. The students in the 1989 Tiananmen protest movement benefited from growing up in a period that on the whole was more open and liberal.

Both of us left China before 1989: I left in 1981, and Ma Xiaodong in 1988, to come to the United States for graduate study. Chinese government's decision to allow students to study abroad showed the country's desire to reconnect herself to the rest of the world. While I missed much of the excitement of the 1980s, Ma Xiaodong was right in the midst of it. She was among a remarkable group of individuals in our generation who were standing at the forefront of China's historic transformation, earnestly promoting economic reform, political liberalization, and cultural openness.

Ye Weili's Story: "Pursue Your Art in Earnest"

YE: The moment I heard the news of the Gang of Four's arrest, I felt a heavy mountain being lifted from my shoulders. My dizziness soon disappeared.

In the new political climate I could do what I had always aspired to do: to pursue a professional career with full devotion. Many years ago when I saw "Sisters on Stage," a line in the film struck a chord in me: "live your life in integrity, pursue your art in earnest." I interpreted this line to mean that one should maintain a clean, honest reputation, and pursue one's life goals with total commitment. The film was criticized during the revolutionizing movement, but I always held that line in my heart. For many years I had covered myself with too many layers of "paint" to be "clean" and my pursuit of a professional career had been blocked. Now that the barricade was removed, I was finally able to follow the desire of my heart.

After graduation from college I was assigned to teach English at Beijing Foreign Language School, a vocational school specializing in teaching foreign languages to secondary school students. Because we had not studied much in college, I felt my English was like a shabby shirt full of holes. I made a self-study plan and spent all my spare time patching up the holes. Now I could study without being accused, I treasured every minute of it. This was a time when the entire society was caught up in a zeal for learning. The popular saying was to make up for the lost time.

English was hot again and nobody was questioning its usefulness. In my first year of teaching the students were elementary school teachers taking a leave from work to learn English. They were expected to teach the language to their students after a year of basic training. I often taught four straight hours without a break. A few young women in my class were fooling around and not taking their studies seriously. I got truly annoyed with them. Why didn't they appreciate this precious opportunity to study? Most of my students worked hard. Some continued their English studies afterward and now are teaching English in high school.

When I first left college I had no idea how to teach. Professor Zhang, my favorite professor at college, told me that "teaching is not a profession. It's an art." My own experience led me to see my role as a conductor of a choir. My job was to make sure that everybody participated in the singing. Eventually I earned the reputation as a good teacher.

After a few years of intensive self-study, I felt I was ready to push my career to a higher level and I was interested in going to graduate school. English was only a tool. I'd like to use it to deepen my pursuit of knowledge. Besides, I didn't like my school. It was a small-minded place where too much time was wasted on trivialities. But I needed permission from the school to take the exams for graduate studies. I talked to the school principal but she wouldn't give me the permission.

I realized I hit a wall here. There was a name for it: work unit ownership. Once you were assigned to work in a specific work unit, it was as if the place owned you. It was particularly bad in elementary and secondary schools, which had difficulty attracting qualified teachers. So my situation was not uncommon.

It was a big setback for me. I was stuck in the school. What should I do? By this time I had married. I figured that if I couldn't go to a graduate school, I might as well become a mother. Perhaps it was time to settle down and focus on family life. Soon I became pregnant. It appeared that life was taking me in a different direction.

During my pregnancy, however, something happened that once again made me strongly want to leave the school. Every year in November my school would move the classes from one-story houses to a four-story building where there was central heating. But the building had no toilets. In November I was well into my pregnancy. I thought about asking the dean's office to give me a classroom in the first floor, so that it would be easier for me to go to an outside toilet. My department had several classrooms on that floor so it should not have been any trouble. But in the end I didn't raise the issue, since I trusted that "*zuzhi*" would do something for me. I had learned from my parents not to make any personal requests, because *zuzhi* (组织 / organization, especially party organization) would take care of things on my behalf. I might have appeared more detached from *zuzhi*—be it the Youth League or the Party—than many of my peers, but deep inside there was this faith in *zuzhi* that had been implanted in me since childhood. Somehow the dean of my school personified *zuzhi* in that institution for me. As it turned out, neither the dean nor the department chair did anything on my behalf. My class was assigned to the top floor.

I've given my own attitude a lot of thought. I realize that the revolution ethos, represented by the notion of *zuzhi*, influenced me more deeply than I had previously thought. This realization has prompted me to ponder the legacy of the revolution and its imprint on me.

MA: But I still don't understand why the dean's office didn't consider your physical conditions. Weren't the leaders always told to care for their subordinates?

YE: The only question the dean asked me, and she asked me several times, was "will you be able to give your students the final exam?" She was concerned because my due day was in mid-January, right around the date set for the final exam. I said, "No problem."

MA: There is a saying that the crying baby always gets fed first. If you don't "cry" they won't pay attention to you. But I still believe most leaders were more considerate than yours.

YE: In any event, soon after we moved to the building, it was clear that I faced a tough situation. During the short break between classes the narrow stairways were filled with students rushing up and down. With my heavy body there was no way I could squeeze myself into the crowd, so I tried not to go to the toilet.

Soon I began to feel not quite right physically. I asked some older teachers and was told that it was normal to feel this way at my stage of pregnancy. So I didn't do anything, until one day I developed a fever of more than 40 degrees centigrade (about 104 degrees Fahrenheit). The doctor said it was caused by a kidney infection. The fever lasted for about a week. I lived in fear before the birth of my child, worried that the fever would have serious consequences for the baby. Luckily my son came out fine. This incident hurt me deeply. I had worked very hard for the school and was known as a good teacher. I felt that the school only used me and didn't care about me as a person. After I recovered from the infection, there were still about 20 days left before my due day. But I decided not to go back to work, which was uncharacteristic of me. I was bitter.

This incident made me determined to leave the school. Soon I thought I got a convincing reason. After my son's birth we moved to a two-bedroom apartment. Living conditions improved but the distance to work was much longer. I had to commute across the entire city to get to work, a trip of about two hours one way. I had a nanny to look after my baby, but there were lots of things for me to take care at home. I found a work place that was much closer to my home: an English language newspaper. But once again my school said "no" to my request to leave.

Around this time the government began to encourage people to study abroad. It was a national policy and an important part of China's opening up endeavor. Work units were not supposed to obstruct their employees from going if they had offers. I got a scholarship from Smith College in the United States. It was like a windfall from the sky. I happened to be introduced to a Smith professor who was looking for Chinese women to recruit for Smith. I became the first student to come to Smith from China since 1949.

I left China in January of 1981, a few days before my son's first birthday. I missed seeing his first steps and hearing his first words. I'm not sure if I would do the same thing today. But at the time this opportunity to study was too good to pass up. I felt a thirst for learning. My so-called college education and the subsequent teaching only sharpened that feeling. It was like giving someone who had long been deprived of water a little amount of the liquid to drink, and it only made that person even thirstier. Now that I was finally able to continue my pursuit of knowledge, how could I let the opportunity pass? Besides, going abroad would be the only way to leave the work unit I disliked.

Believe it or not, when I was making the decision to go abroad, I thought about my village in northern Shanxi and the peasants there. I guess I needed a larger reason to justify my leaving behind my baby. I always felt I owed my village and the people there something. Somehow, at some point in my life, I'd like to do something for them. I told myself that going abroad to study would equip me with modern knowledge and make me better able to help them. That was how I felt then. I thought I was going away for only a year, which was the duration of the Smith scholarship. At the time I definitely planned to return to China after my study. My family was going to be in three different countries—my son remaining in China, my husband working for a Chinese trade company in Canada, and I in America.

The hardest thing was to leave my son and my mother. I got up very early on the day of my departure. My son was still fast asleep. I gave him a light kiss and quickly turned away, lest my tears came. My mother saw me off outside our home. In the cold winter morning she followed our car, limping along the quiet street, her gray hair flying in the wind.

Ma Xiaodong's Story: The Midwife for "Pan Xiao"

MA: When you left China in early 1981, I was working as a reporter for the journal *Chinese Youth*, the official organ of the Communist Youth League. I began my work there in May 1979, soon after I returned to Beijing from Heilongjiang. The country was breaking free from the shackles of the Cultural Revolution, and people, especially the young, were dying for a change. *Chinese Youth* was in the vanguard for "emancipation of the mind," earnestly voicing the concerns and demands of young people and ardently promoting new ideas. I worked at the journal for nine years, throwing myself passionately into this great cause. I regard this period as the high point of my life.

The political change since the late 1970s generated a great deal of tension within society. The press became an important medium for conveying the complaints, confusion and longings of ordinary citizens, something that would have been unthinkable in the previous era. During the 1980s I participated in a number of public debates sponsored by my journal. The most memorable one was the Pan Xiao discussion (潘晓讨论).

YE: You were part of it? It was probably the best-known public discussion in the 1980s. You interviewed Pan Xiao?

MA: Pan Xiao was not a person. We combined the surname of one individual and the given name of another to come up with this pen name. But you might say Pan Xiao represented millions of Chinese youth who felt frustrated with the weight of the old way of thinking still prevalent in society.

As a national youth journal, we were aware that there existed a great deal of discontent among the young. Everyday we received letters from our readers voicing complaints, exposing injustices, and seeking advice. Take clothing as an example. Many young people stopped wearing drab Mao jackets and started experimenting with more stylish clothes, which often reflected a Western influence. Some even donned baggy trousers. Conservative-minded people frowned upon such change. In a few extreme cases we were aware of, some work units even set up stations at the gates to check what employees wore.

In the early 1980s, our journal held discussion meetings in a number of schools, factories, and neighborhoods to encourage young people to speak out. At one such meeting, half the audience cried. Many pointed out the gap between the high-sounding ideals disseminated by the government and their everyday reality. They were told to work for the realization of a communist society, but that goal was remote and disconnected from the problems they confronted in daily life.

During one such meeting, a colleague and I discovered a man and a woman, Pan Yi and Huang Xiaojue. We asked them to write down their thoughts. Huang Xiaojue wrote something I still remember by heart:

> "The sun is shining because of the way it is, not because its purpose is to shed light on us people on the earth. Like the sun, if each of us takes care of his or her own business and tries to fulfill his or her own potential, the end result will be that the entire human society benefits. Subjectively, we are all for ourselves; objectively, we help others."

This was very different from the kind of education we received in the past. We had been taught to sacrifice our personal interests for the greater good. What Huang wrote made me think about our education more critically.

YE: She hit the nail on the head: how did an individual's interests fare in our society? What I experienced during my pregnancy made me wonder about similar issues.

MA: In many ways I identified with these young people. Huang Xiaojue was very unhappy with her situation. As an idealist, she encountered many constraints in life. In the piece she wrote for us, she cried out, "Why is the life path getting narrower and narrower?" This line became the title of our article.

YE: Your article?

MA: Huang and Pan's original writings were too long. We had to condense them into one shorter piece. I was assigned the job. So I was sort of the mid-wife of the Pan Xiao article. After it was published, letters from readers began pouring in. Many were addressed to Pan Xiao. So much mail was coming in everyday that the post office had to deliver the mail in a special van. Many people also called. More than one identified himself / herself as "Pan Xiao." We soon opened a special column to invite public discussion. For a while it seemed as if the entire society was participating in the discussion. The journal enjoyed the national spotlight and Pan Xiao became a household name. In the end we received a total of over 6,000 letters from readers across the country. The discussion also attracted attention from abroad. All the major news agencies in the world reported it. I think this was the most glorious moment in *Chinese Youth's* history of 30 years.

As I think about it now, the timing was critical for this article to stir up such an enormous response. This was when thoughtful Chinese realized that as a lesson drawn from the Cultural Revolution, we should emphasize the value of humanism and try to establish a society that respected the rights of each individual citizen. The Pan Xiao discussion struck a ready chord.

The 1980s was a conflict-ridden decade. The conservatives within the party didn't like the tone of the discussion and accused it of representing bourgeois liberalism. For a while the journal was under heavy pressure. But the discussion has stood the test of time. Recently, the Chinese central TV station showed a special program commemorating the twentieth anniversary of China's opening-up and reform (1978–1998). Among the major events of the 1980s, the Pan Xiao discussion was mentioned, and the signatures of the editors in charge of the discussion were displayed on the screen. Mine was among them.

YE: You've left an imprint on history.

MA: The 1980s witnessed transformations on many fronts. We've mentioned what happened to people's dress. I myself also underwent interesting change in this area. For a long time after the fall of the Gang of Four I continued to wear simple plain clothes, even when many women around me had shed their unisex outfits. I was slow to change.

In 1984, I was asked to report the visit of a youth delegation from Japan and accompany its travel throughout China. To the surprise of my superiors I turned down this honorable assignment. I didn't tell them why, but an assignment like this would require proper clothes, which I didn't have. At my superiors' insistence, I finally agreed to the assignment and started to prepare for the trip. A friend took me to a fashion designer and said she might be able to lend me some clothes. The designer showed me her closet, which contained many beautiful outfits. My eyes shone.

After I chose a few outfits, the woman advised me on what color shoes should go with the clothes, what accessories to wear, and so on. In the end she also did my makeup. Afterward, I looked in the mirror and couldn't believe my eyes. The dress fit me as though it were cut just for me. I was even more amazed by the effect of the light makeup. It made such a big difference. That night I almost wore the makeup to bed.

YE: Didn't you always have a fascination with beauty as a little girl? It was being woken up in you now.

MA: That's true. Nowadays I pay more attention to what I wear and how I look, but I have to say I disagree with the view that women of our generation never looked beautiful. My favorite photos are still the ones taken when I was in Yunnan.

YE: There is always something precious in one's youth, especially if it's our own.

MA: I'd like to switch to a heavy topic: my mother's death. It happened in 1981 when she died from lung cancer. By the time it was diagnosed, it was too late. She spent her last days in a hospital and we all took turns caring for her. Relatives, friends, and colleagues all came to see her, some from thousands of miles away. The number of visitors surprised other patients in the same ward. One visitor was the principal of my mother's school. During the Cultural Revolution, my mother refused to denounce him despite the heavy pressure she was under. At my mother's funeral, the old man recalled this incident with tears in his eyes.

One evening before my mother's death, my father and I happened to be by her bedside. My mother was in deep sleep. In a low voice, as if talking to himself, my father said, "What your mother and I have had is true love." I was astonished and deeply touched. This was the first time I'd heard the word "love" spoken by my father, the son of a peasant and a veteran Communist Party member.

I had just turned 30 at the time of my mother's death. I was already married but my son was not yet born. My husband was a *zhiqing* from Shanghai and I got to know him when I was in Heilongjiang. The children of my two brothers had received love from my mother. My son, Niuniu, was the only grandchild she never saw. How I wish my mother could have lived to see Niuniu!

YE: I always wish that my son, Yuanyuan, could have gotten to know my mother better. Just as we never got to know our grandparents, our children also don't really know theirs. It seems that a new round of generational disjunction is repeating itself.

MA: This is indeed the case.

When I went back to work after my maternity leave, I received a promotion. My new job kept me in the office rather than going out on assignments. I became restless after a while, feeling that I had lost touch with real life. I asked to be a reporter again and my request was approved. Some of my colleagues didn't understand my decision, but I knew I did the right thing.

As a reporter, I got to travel to many parts of China. My experiences as a *zhiqing* both in Yunnan and Heilongjiang had familiarized me with rural poverty. My job as a reporter further drew my attention to problems in this area. Once I visited a country school in a poor region in northern Shaanxi province and the visit has left an indelible impression on me.

This was the only middle school in the region, and the majority of the students were children of local peasants. When I arrived in the school, classes were already over for the day and the kids had gone to a nearby town to play. I had passed through the town earlier in the day and had found nothing interesting there: all it had was a few shops, a post office, and some restaurants. But to the kids it was the most exciting place. While waiting for their return I peeped into their dorms. I saw mugs lining the windowsill, but I didn't find any toothbrushes. I asked why and was told that the students didn't brush their teeth because the region never had a sufficient supply of water. I then went to their canteen, where each student had a storage box for grains and salted vegetables. Once every two weeks they would go home to fetch a fresh supply of food.

It was already quite dark when the kids came back from town. I saw them running toward the school, laughing and talking loudly. Almost all of them were boys. Looking at their faces, I suddenly imagined that my son Niuniu was among them. Then I asked myself, how would you feel if your son ate salted vegetables everyday and didn't get to brush his teeth? This thought made my heartache and I didn't want to think about it any further.

The kids quieted down when they saw me. They were shy in front of a stranger and they looked at me with curiosity. To make conversation, I asked to see where they slept and they took me into their dorm, which was a deep cave room. It was already dark and there was no electricity. Under the dim light I saw a long *kang* (brick platform bed) from one end of the cave to the other. It must have been very crowded at night for the many boys. In the dorm, each boy kept a small box for cooked food. I asked them what food their parents had prepared for them. By now it was completely dark and I was unable to see anything. The kids competed with each other to invite me to feel their food. So I used my hand to touch. I didn't think I touched anything better than bread made of corn and millet.

Next morning I said good-bye to the kids and went back to Beijing. I wrote an article about how students in a country school pursued their studies under hard conditions. I have always wanted to tell my son about this visit. But I have been afraid that my son would have no clue as to what I was talking about, since the world of those kids in rural China was a far cry from his life in Boston. I would feel hurt if he didn't understand. So I have said nothing. I'd still like my son to know someday.

YE: Same here. I hope someday I can take my son to visit my village.

YE: In August of 1988, I left Beijing with my son to come to the United States. My husband had been in Boston for a year as a graduate student at Northeastern University and he was waiting for us to join him. After our airplane took off from the Beijing airport, my six-year-old son suddenly said, "Finally we are in the blue sky." He sounded like a grown-up reciting a poem. I didn't feel poetic. I didn't know what was waiting for me in a strange new land.

Afterword

An Update about Us

After receiving her doctoral degree in sociology from Northeastern University in 1999, Ma Xiaodong went back to China and now teaches at Fudan University in Shanghai. Her concern for rural China and women's issues, amply demonstrated in the preceding pages, has been reflected both in her Ph.D. thesis and her current research in China. The former involved a study of a village in Jiangsu province during the reform era and the latter has centered on rural poverty and women's reproductive health. She spends several months every year doing fieldwork in the same county in northern Shaanxi where years ago she visited as a journalist. Living over ten years in the United States has not made her forget that part of China. Some of her colleagues in Shanghai are puzzled by her decision to do research in such an impoverished region. This book helps explain the draw of rural China to her.

I received my Ph.D. from Yale University in 1989 and now teach Chinese history and women's studies at the University of Massachusetts at Boston. My doctoral thesis was about an earlier generation of Chinese youth who had come to study in the United States in the first decades of the twentieth century. Totally ignorant about those people who had come before me, and who, as I found out, had contributed enormously to China's effort to modernize after returning home, I started digging up long-buried materials about their experiences in America. The result of my "rescue" endeavor is the monograph *Seeking Modernity in China's Name: Chinese Students in the United States 1900–1927*, published by Stanford University in 2001.

As a student of history, I am keenly aware of the repeated loss and distortion of memory in twentieth-century China, either in the name of progress and "forward-lookingness" (向前看 / *xiang qian kan*) or for the sake of political correctness. The long suppression and marginalization of the early generation of American-educated Chinese is a case in point. I have tried—in my first monograph, in this collaborative memoir, and in my current research project—to repossess lost memories, to connect "dots" in history, and to extract meanings. I am presently studying a cohort of urban educated youth who joined the Chinese communist forces at the outbreak of the Sino-Japanese War. Careful readers of this book will recognize my personal connection to this generation of Communist Party intellectuals, since my parents belong to the same group.

Together, these projects will make a trilogy that spans three distinctive generations in roughly one hundred years of the eventful and at times tumultuous twentieth-century Chinese history. As a member of the youngest generation, I am intimately linked to the two proceeding generations. While the early band of American-educated students were my predecessors in China's century-long quest for modernization, I have more than a blood connection to my parents' generation. Close scrutiny of my youthful years has made me more aware of the deep imprint the revolution ethos has left on me. By studying the party intellectuals I'd like to look into the mixed legacy of the Chinese revolution. Once again, a great deal of sorting out needs to be done.

My Generation

China has changed so much in the last 25 years that I sometimes feel I am a stranger in my homeland, even though I frequently visit my family there. My home city of Beijing has undergone such a thorough "face lift" that more than once I have become lost in the midst of brand new high-rise buildings. Gone are the familiar scenes such as a neighborhood stationery shop, now replaced by a fancy department store. The bond I still feel with my native city is mostly through people, especially friends from my school and countryside days. They are people of my generation.

It is noteworthy that the countryside years have become a focal point in history to my peers in China. In fact, it is largely because of the shared experience in those years that a strong generational identity has been forged among people in our age cohort. A literary genre, called *zhiqing* writing, emerged in the 1980s, created by writers who spent years as educated youth themselves.

In contrast to the abundance of reminiscence about the *zhiqing* period, very little has been written about the experiences of Red Guards.[1] While not everyone was once a Red Guard and not every Red Guard committed atrocities, a considerable number of the young people did take part in violent acts at the height of the Cultural Revolution. Yet after nearly 40 years that phase of the Cultural Revolution has remained a sore spot very few people from my generation have been willing to touch.

The tendency to escape from the memory of that horrible time exists in the Chinese society at large. While it goes beyond the scope of this book to address the complex reasons behind the phenomenon, suffice it to say that an honest probing of the horrors of the Cultural Revolution cannot avoid looking squarely into the structural flaws in the political system and the personal responsibilities of Mao Zedong, an undertaking that is still not feasible in the political climate of today's China.

Still the question remains how each individual who participated in violence should face his or her own moral issues. Working on this memoir has made the question acquire more weight for me, and has made me acutely aware of our huge collective silence. This is a question members of my generation need to confront. We owe it to history *and* to our posterity to do so. We have had a bad enough experience trying to straighten up distorted records about much of the twentieth-century history that happened before our time, we don't want to put our children in the same historical predicament. As a generation we have proved that we were capable of regenerating ourselves despite the adversities of the Cultural Revolution. Let us show that we can face the history in ourselves.

I will not forget the moment in our conversation when Ma Xiaodong started talking about her participation in hitting a woman during the Anti-four-olds Campaign. I could sense the tremendous uneasiness and pain the topic was causing her. Later I realized how extremely difficult it must have been for her to disclose the matter, in light of what happened to her own mother only a few days after she beat that woman. I was touched by her courage to face a deeply hurtful past.

Ma Xiaodong's participation in this project led her to want to know more about what happened to her mother on that horrible August day. Finally, in 1999, her father let her read his reminiscence of the day, written retrospectively in the early 1980s soon after his wife's death. For the first time after more than 30 years Mao Xiaodong found out the details of her mother's suffering. What shook her the most was the emotional side of the episode— her mother's feelings, her father's crying—a whole dimension she was totally unaware of at the time. The emotional aspect is a vital part of any living history, and it is the most human and often the most powerful, yet it frequently gets buried. One wonders how much is still hidden or has been permanently lost from history about the Cultural Revolution.

As a follow-up to my inquiry into the death of Bian Zhongyun, I conducted two small group interviews of my secondary school classmates in the summer of 2002. I wanted to know what they remembered about the death and how it affected them. It happened that most of them came from families considered non-red at the outset of the Cultural Revolution, some being downright "black." This was the first time since 1966 that classmates sat together talking about that unforgettable summer. Some recounted what they witnessed on the day of Bian's death; others instead told of injustices imposed on to members of their own families. Several cried hard. Almost four decades had since passed yet the wounds had not truly healed. Their stories and observations greatly humbled me and allowed me to understand the summer of 1966 from new perspectives. Perhaps we need more gatherings like this, among people who were pigeonholed in different political categories during the Cultural Revolution, to exchange long-buried memories and to share long-repressed emotions. This would be a necessary first step in helping us heal from the trauma of the Cultural Revolution.

Several of my classmates had already retired, which was not surprising to me. It is well-known in China that a large number of people from my generation, whose education was forever interrupted as a result of the Cultural Revolution, have retired at a fairly early age. While it is true that some prominent leadership posts in today's China are held by individuals in my age group, it has also become increasingly clear that many of my peers have found themselves in a disadvantaged position in the current market-oriented and credential-crazed economy. This reality has led more than one observer to note that the long-term negative impact of the "up to the mountains and down to the countryside" movement has only begun to be felt.[2] While there are people who consider their rural experience beneficial to them personally and perhaps also professionally, there are many others who regard the years spent in the countryside as a waste of their precious youth, and attribute their present unsatisfactory situation to their earlier loss of formal education.

With our expanded educational opportunities both in China and abroad, Ma Xiaodong and I belong to a tiny fraction of very lucky people in our generation. Bearing this in mind, I constantly remind myself to appreciate my good fortune. Ma Xiaodong, meanwhile, has clearly decided to apply the knowledge she acquired in the United States to help people who most need attention in today's China: peasant men and women, especially women, in poverty-stricken regions. In a piece she has been working on entitled "Yellow Earth, Let Me Talk to You" (黄土地, 我对你说 / huang tudi, wo dui ni shuo), she identifies herself as a female sociologist and writes about the conditions of rural women empathetically. Marriage for sale is still a common practice in the villages she has conducted her fieldwork. In the native language, marrying a daughter is simply called "selling a daughter." Among several young women she has interviewed, there is one who was betrothed at the age of 15 and another at 14.[3] When the girl in the latter case expressed her unwillingness to leave home, she was told by her family that if they didn't marry her off, they wouldn't be able to get a wife for her brother. The third woman told Ma Xiaodong that when she was nine, she had summoned courage to ask her father to let her go to school, only to be told that the family had no money to support her education. Now all she hopes is that her parents will choose a reasonable family for her, that her future mother-in-law will be kind and her husband a decent man.

In many ways these are the same old stories familiar to me when I lived in rural northern Shanxi more than three decades ago. I am surprised that things have changed so little. While urban coastal China has greatly shortened its gap with the developed world, a considerable proportion of interior rural China has continuously fallen behind. At a time when many people in urban China are busy pursuing a good material life, individuals like Ma Xiaodong are rare and deserve admiration. Here with her almost dogged idealism, a commitment to social justice, and a never wavering belief in the larger good, Ma Xiaodong represents my generation at its best.

History as Wellspring

We began this project in the mid-1990s when the twentieth century, often described as calamitous for the world as a whole, was drawing to a close. The end of the fierce cold war and the triumphant ascendancy of global capitalism led some people to proclaim that history had reached an "end."[4] There was hence no need to search for new solutions to mankind's problems, as history already had provided the final verdict.

Now facing a world ridden with increased racial and ethnic tension, heightened religious hatred, revived imperialist impulse, globalized exploitation, alarming economic disparity, persistent gender inequality, and a rapidly worsening natural environment, more and more people have come to realize that we actually have entered a new age of grave uncertainty.

Can history be of any help? Can we see it not as a decree, or a curse, or a burden, but as a mirror, and a resource? Should history help open up rather than close off our minds, regenerate rather than stifle our imagination?

History by nature is messy. Take my generation as an example. In many ways it personified the aspirations, contradictions, and serious defects of the Mao era. In our attempt to understand how that era shaped us, we try in this book to sort out the entangled history and to balance a critical scrutiny of the period with a sweeping negation of it—a very fine line to walk. Only by doing so can the historical past serve as a meaningful lesson for the future.

A debate has been going on in today's China regarding how to evaluate women's liberation during the Mao years. The women of my generation are the locus of the debate. Should we be praised for having greatly enhanced women's presence in the public realm and for having proven ourselves equal to men in abundant instances, or should we be pitied for having suffered severe deprivation of femininity in our youth?

Either case can be argued, as the stories of Ma Xiaodong and my own show. The task is to carefully inspect the messed-up baggage, so to speak, so as to know what to get rid of and what to keep. The painstaking process of reviewing our early lives has enabled Ma Xiaodong and me to achieve a more balanced understanding of our experience growing up female in the PRC. Ultimately both of us are thankful that the ideal of gender equality (though without gender consciousness) was firmly implanted earlier in our lives. It has helped us greatly in our later lives both in China and in the United States.

Tremendous change has taken place in the lives of Chinese women since the reform era began in the late 1970s. To some extent the young urban women have undergone a dazzling transformation from tough iron girls to sexy Shanghai babies.[5] A more open and tolerant attitude toward female sexuality has benefited women in many ways, but has also led to, in numerous other cases, exploitation of women as sexual objects. Against this backdrop, there is an earnest need to reaffirm the positive aspects of women's liberation during the revolutionary and socialist periods and to use them as the foundation for further endeavors to better women's lives in today's China.

Participating in this oral history and memoirist writing has made me more capable of viewing history as a wellspring of resources. Two scenes from the lives of my paternal grandmother and my mother respectively strike me with special power and meaning: my grandmother knelt down in front of *taitai* thanking for a red dress to wear in her death; my mother sunbathed her crippled leg in front of a cave in Yan'an. They both are my history. Women's lives have never been easy, in China and elsewhere, yet I realize I have come a long way from my grandmother's days when concubinage was common place, thanks to the brave women and men in the course of the twentieth century to push for the betterment of women's lives in China. I am proud that my mother was among them, despite the fact that the ideal of gender equality was not quite fulfilled in her life. But the ideal persisted for her, and boiled down to this message she passed on to me: as a woman, you must strive hard to stand tall.

Working on this book has been a self-discovering and self-strengthening process for me. I now know where I can draw support if I am cornered in life. I am grateful that I can turn to my remarkable family, to the stories of my resilient generation, and to the long and hardy twentieth-century Chinese history for strength and inspiration. By knowing where I came from, both in a narrow, familial way and in a broad, historical sense, I feel I am now more solidly anchored as a person and a woman to face an increasingly complex and murky world.

Every person in our generation has a story. Ours are neither special nor striking. But they are part of a larger history. While being individual and personal, they offer slices of Chinese life that mirror the incredible history in the second half of twentieth-century China. Just as Ma Xiaodong realized years later that she could have learned something from the life of her paternal grandfather, I hope our sons, Yuanyuan and Niuniu, who have both grown up in the United States, will learn something from their mothers' lives in China.

Glossary

Selected Chinese Terms	Pinyin	English Translation
大串联	dachuanlian	great linkup
单位	danwei	work unit
大院	dayuan	compound
黑帮	heibang	black gangster
胡同	hutong	alleyway
集体	jiti	the collective
牛鬼蛇神	niugui sheshen	ox ghosts and snake spirits
四合院	siheyuan	squared dwelling
铁姑娘	tieguniang	iron girls
逍遥派	xiaoyaopai	bystander
知青	zhiqing	educated youth
走资派	zouzipai	people who take the capitalist road
组织	zuzhi	party organization

Famous personages

Deng Xiaoping CCP leader; accused of being the No.2 person "who took the capitalist road" in the early years of the Cultural Revolution; regarded as China's "paramount leader" in the reform era; died in 1997.

Jiang Qing Mao's wife; radical Cultural Revolution leader; a leading member of the "Gang of Four"; committed suicide in 1991.

Liu Shaoqi Head of the state until 1966; accused of being the No.1 person "who took the capitalist road" during the Cultural Revolution; died a sad death in 1969.

Mao Zedong   Chairman of the CCP; responsible for the launching of the Cultural Revolution; died in 1976.

Peng Dehuai   PRC's Minister of Defense until dismissed from the post in 1959 after the Lushan Conference; died in 1974.

Zhou Enlai   PRC's premier until his death in 1976.

Notes

Introduction

1. Some of these works are Jung Chang's *Wild Swans: Three Daughters of China* (New York: Doubleday, 1991), Nien Cheng's *Life and Death in Shanghai* (New York: Penguin, 1986), Archee Min's *Red Azalea* (New York: Pantheon Books, 1994), Nanchu's *Red Sorrow, A Memoir* (New York: Arcade, 2001), Ningkun Wu's *A Single Tear* (New York: The Atlantic Monthly Press, 1993), Liang Heng's *Son of Revolution* (New York: Vintage, 1984), Zi-ping Luo's *A Generation Lost* (New York: Avon, 1990), and Yuan Gao's *Born Red* (Stanford, CA: Stanford University Press, 1987). Ray Yang's memoir, *Spider Eaters* (Berkeley, CA: University of California Press, 1997), offers a more balanced and especially reflective account of her life in China. Please also see Zhong Xueping, et al. eds. *Some of Us: Chinese Women Growing Up in the Mao Era* (New Brunswick, NJ: Rutgers University Press, 2001). It is a collection of short memoirs written by a group of Chinese women growing up in the Mao era and now living in the United States. It offers nuanced and complex portrayals of life in the Mao era that challenges the stereotypes of persecution and repression in Mao China.
2. One exception is Lao Gui's book, *Xue Yu Huo* [*Blood and Fire*] (Beijing: Zhongguo shehui kexueyuan cubanshe, 1998), which offers a rare account of the author's experience during the Cultural Revolution as a Red Guard, including his participation in violence.
3. In recent years I have paid several visits to my dead school leader's husband, Mr. Wang Jingyao, and have held in-depth conversations with the old man.
4. On the many studies and theories about student behavior, see, for instance, Emily Honig, "Maoist Mappings of Gender: Reassessing the Red Guards," in *Chinese Femininities/Chinese Masculinities*, eds. Susan Brownell and Jeffery Wasserstrom (Berkeley, CA: University of California Press, 2002), pp.255–268. The article looks at gender as a way to explain the violence of female students. Also see Lin Chun, "Love and Hate: Learning 'Human Nature' under Communism," in *Science, Politics and Social Practices: Essays on Marxism and Science, Philosophy of Culture and the Social Science*, ed. Kostas Gavroglo et al. (Kluwer Academic Publishers, 1995), which looks at both gender and education as the ways to explain violence committed by young people during the

Cultural Revolution. For the early phase of the Cultural Revolution and how violence featured in it, also see Wang Shaoguang, "Between Destruction and Construction: the First Year of the Cultural Revolution" and Lynn White and Kan-yee Law, "Explanations for China's Revolution at its Peak," both in *The Chinese Cultural Revolution Reconsidered*, edited by Kam-yee Law (New York: Palgrave MacMillan, 2003). Among books in Chinese on the subject of violence and explanations for it, see *Canque de chuanglanban* [*Broken Window Frames*], ed. Li Hui (Shenzhen: Haitian chubanshe, 1998). Please also see the documentary film, *Morning Sun*, Long Bow Group, 2003. It contains interviews of a number of Chinese who participated and experienced the Cultural Revolution and now reflect upon that turbulent time. Among the interviewees are some prominent Beijing secondary school Red Guard leaders during the early stage of the Cultural Revolution.

5. Anita Chan, *Children of Mao: Personality Development and Political Activism in the Red Guard Generation* (Seattle, WA: University of Washington Press, 1985) pp.183–184.

6. The documentary film *Morning Sun* notes this important shift. See the section on "Unlearning." Also see Ray Yang's discussion on "exposing the third layer of thoughts," *Spider Eaters*, pp.97–100.

7. Key schools referred to those that were academically competitive. They required high scores in entrance examinations to get in.

8. Among the many works on trauma and recovery, please see in particular, Judith Herman, *Trauma and Recovery: the Aftermath of Violence from Domestic Abuse to Political Terror* (NY, New York: Basic Books, 1997), which has a chapter on the various stages a person goes through in order to recover from a past trauma. Doing oral history is an effective way of confronting past incidents that otherwise would be buried in memories. See Donald Ritchie, *Doing Oral History* (Prinston, NJ: Oxford University Press, 2003) p.46.

9. This view is best represented in Jonathan Mirsky's article "China's Wasted Half-Century: Nothing to Celebrate," in *The New Republic*, October 1999, pp.30–35.

10. There have been some writings in Chinese on this elusive topic. See, for instance, Du Xinxin, "pai pozi kaozheng" ["The Origin of 'pai pozi' "], and Bei Suni, "piaopai shiling: linglei weigeshi" ["Miscellaneous Accounts on the Bystanders"]. Both can be found in www.edubridge.com. Also see Pan Qing, *Shuqing nianhua* [*The Lyric Years*] (Beijing: Zuojia chubanshe, 2002).

11. Peter Zarrow, "Meanings of Cultural Revolution: Memoirs of Exile," *Positions*, 7:1, 1999, pp.165–190.

12. This view is expressed by Francis Fukuyama. See his *The End of History and the Last Man* (Perennial, reprint edition, 1993).

13. I see three basic rounds of sweeping historical negation in twentieth-century China. The first occurred during the May Fourth new cultural movement that began around mid-1910s and lasted into the 1920s. Chinese tradition,

symbolized by Confucianism, was categorically denounced and there was the suggestion for a wholesale "Westernization." The second round took place after the founding of the PRC. History books that followed the party line suppressed, marginalized, and distorted events and personnel that were not part of the Chinese Communist Party-led revolution. Our grandparents, as members of "exploiting classes", were wiped out from historical memory. The third round has been going strong in the West in recent years, particularly since the 1990s after the end of the cold war. The Mao era has received a flatly negative portrayal, exemplified by a number of Chinese memoirs published in the West. Meanwhile, the history of the CCP-led revolution is also under critical scrutiny, which I believe is necessary. There is, however, the tendency to replace the "revolution paradigm" with "modernization paradigm" and to question the very necessity of the revolution. This revisionist trend has also expressed itself in China, albeit more implicitly.

14. Ritchie argues that "Oral history is about asking questions," see, *Doing Oral History*, p.46.

Chapter One   "Even If You Cut It, It Will Not Come Apart"

1. Li Zehou and Liu Zaifu, *Gaobie geming* [*Farewell to Revolution*] (Hong Kong: Tiandi tushu, 1995).
2. It was the official new agency of the CCP before 1949 and has been the official news agency of the PRC since 1949.
3. A type of romantic and sentimental literature popular from the beginning of the twentieth century to the 1930s. It appealed particularly to urban residents.
4. This observation was made by my fifth uncle Ye Duzhuang in the 1990s.
5. I want to thank my cousin Ye Wa for this information. It was told to her by my third uncle Ye Duyi in the mid 1990s. Even though more than 60 years had passed and my uncle was an old man in his eighties, he cried hard like a baby when recounting this scene.
6. His name was Zhang Boling, the principal of the Nankai School. He was one of the most prominent educators of his generation. He came to study in the United States in the early twentieth century and received a degree in education from the Teachers' College of Columbia University.
7. On this movement, please see John Israel, *Student Nationalism in China 1927–1937* (Stanford, CA: Stanford University Press, 1966).
8. It was an effort of Mao Zedong and his trusted colleagues to cleanse the Communist Party to get rid of so-called spies for the Nationalists. Many educated youth from urban areas were under investigation. Some were detained. In the case of my father, he was detained for 3 years. Most people were eventually rehabilitated, but the campaign left a dark shadow on their

memory. On the political campaign, see, among other works, Gao Hua, *Hong taiyang shi zenyang shengqide: Yan'an zhengfeng yundong de lailong qumai* [How the "Red Sun" Arose: The Origin and the Legacy of the Rectification Campaign in Yan'an] (Hong Kong: The Chinese University Press, 2000); David Apter & Tony Saich, *Revolutionary Discourse in Mao's Republic* (Cambridge, MA: Harvard University Press, 1994).

9. Land Reform in China took place in the late 1940s and early 1950s under the leadership of the Communist Party. One outcome of the Land Reform was to classify the rural population in five main categories: landlord, rich peasant, middle peasant, poor peasant, and tenant peasant. Those in the first two categories were considered members of the exploiting class.

10. Lu Xun (1881–1936), one of the most prominent writers in twentieth-century China. His bitter critique of Confucianism and the old society influenced generations of young Chinese.

Chapter Two "Flowers of the Nation"

1. When I saw the Disney production of the animated film "The Little Mermaid," I was disappointed. I thought it lacked the profound humanist touch I found the most moving in Anderson's original tale.

2. Liu Hulan was a peasant girl in Shanxi province. She joined the communists at a very young age. When she was killed by the local Nationalist force in December 1946, she was barely 15 years old. Her story became well-known to the Chinese children in the 1950s.

3. Movies that were very likely produced by countries of the capitalist West and therefore were politically problematic. They were not distributed commercially in movie theatres.

4. One stroke is for a leader at the "platoon" level, two strokes for a leader at the "company" level, and three strokes for a leader at the "brigade" level.

5. Homeroom teacher, or *ban zhuren* in Chinese, plays a more comprehensive role in the academic and social life of a student in the Chinese elementary and secondary school educational system. In many ways this role resembles that of a counselor.

6. Du Fu (712–770) was a poet in Tang dynasty. Su Dongbo (1037–1101) and Xin Qiji (1140–1207) both lived in Song dynasty. Their poems represent the highest level of classical Chinese poetry.

7. Beginning in the second half of 1960, when the food situation became severe in the cities, cadres ranked 17 and above began to get one *jin* of sugar and two *jin* of soybeans per month. Those ranked 13 and above would get an extra two *jin* of meat and two *jin* of eggs, and those ranked 9 and above would get four *jin* of meat. There were a total of 24 ranks in the system.

8. The Democratic League was formed in the early 1940s. It aspired to represent a "third path" different from either the Nationalist Party or the Communist

Party. It became increasingly pro-communists in the last years of the Nationalist rule. Members of the Democratic League were hit very hard during the Anti-rightist Campaign in 1957. Roughly one-sixth of its members were denounced as rightists.

9. The Zhang-Luo Anti-Party Alliance referred to an alleged alliance between Zhang Bojun and Luo Lonji—both held leadership positions within the Democratic League. The charge was totally groundless.

10. Peng Dehuai was the Minister of Defense in the 1950s. In 1959, at a conference of the CCP Central Committee held in Lushan, Jiangxi province, Peng criticized the Great Leap Forward as "hot-headed" that had caused damage to the economy and people's livelihood. Mao Zedong took the critique as an attack against his authority and accused Peng of being "anti-party." Peng was dismissed from his position in the government and the party.

11. In the late 1970s most rightists were rehabilitated, leaving only a handful with the black label. But the Anti-rightist Campaign was still deemed necessary by the CCP even though it admitted that the vast majority of the rightists were wrongly persecuted.

12. *Wuzhong Qiyuan* [*The Origin of Species*], by Charles Darwin, translated by Zhou Jianren, Ye Duzhuang, and Fang Zongxi, (Beijing: Commercial Press, 1993). Afterword to the new edition by Ye Duzhuang.

Chapter Three   From Paper Crown to Leather Belt

*I want to thank Prof. Vera Schwarcz of Wesleyan University for the suggestion of this title.

1. On March 18, 1926, over 40 students and citizens in Beijing were gunned down by warlord government troops during a demonstration. Among the dead there were some students from the Beijing Women's Normal College where Lu Xun taught. These young female students became famous martyrs because of an article Lu Xun wrote to commemorate their deaths.

2. The official organ of the Chinese Communist Party. The paper's editorials conveyed the voice of the party.

3. Mao Zedong, "Notes on the Report of the Investigation of the Beijing Teachers' Training College," July 3, 1965.

4. "Red categories" referred to those people who came from families of revolutionary martyrs, revolutionary cadres, revolutionary army men, workers, and (former) poor and lower-middle peasants.

5. "Five black categories" referred to those who came from families of former landlords, former rich peasants, "reactionaries," "bad elements," and "rightists."

6. Many years later when I saw this classmate again I told her about my impression of her that day. She burst out crying. She told me that the reason for her black status was her "counter-revolutionary" father, whom she had hardly known in her childhood because he had been in prison ever since she was a

little girl. She might have appeared calm to me during our encounter that day, but deep inside she was filled with despair.

7. Communist Youth League is a youth organization under the leadership of the Chinese Communist Party. Young people between the ages 15 and 25 are eligible to join.

8. The lines come from Mao's poem "Inscription on a Photograph of Militia Women," (*wei nüminbing tizhao*), written in 1961 and first published in 1963. One translation of the poem can be found in *Poems of Mao Zedong*, translated by Gu Zhengkun (Beijing: Peking University Press, 1993), p.171.

9. Paul is the main character in Nikolay Ostrovsky's novel *How the Steel Was Tempered*, trans. Mei Yi (Huadong Xinhua Shudian: 1947). The book is about the struggle between the red army and the white army during the Russia's civil war in the late 1910s. Gadfly is the main character in the novel *The Gadfly*, written by E. L. Voynich, (Indypublish.com, 2002).

10. I want to thank Zhu Hong for the translation of this line.

11. A famous Chinese artist, Xu Beihong was trained in France in the 1920s.

12. In his July 3, 1965 directive on the educational system, Mao wrote, "Students are heavily loaded [with work] and their health suffers. Their study therefore becomes useless. [I] suggest a cut of one third of their total activities."

13. Sending work teams to take over the leadership of a given place was a customary practice of the Chinese Communist Party. Land Reform of the late 1940s and early 1950s, for instance, was conducted by work teams sent to various rural localities.

14. Liu Shaoqi was the president of the state and No.2 person in the party. Deng Xiaoping was the party general secretary. They were in Beijing in early June when the Cultural Revolution suddenly erupted on many school campuses. Mao stayed in the south at this time.

15. A couplet consists of two consecutive lines of verses, equal in length and with rhyme. In most of the cases it contains lines that express good wishes and positive feelings. Occasionally, like the couplet mentioned here, it is used to denounce people.

16. Mao Zedong, "Report on an Investigation of the Peasant Movement in Hunan," *Selected Works of Mao Zedong*, I, p.28. (Article originally written in March, 1927.) Quoted in *Quotations from Chairman Mao Tsetung* (Beijing: Foreign Languages Press, 1972).

17. I want to thank Mr. Wang Jingyao, husband of Bian Zhongyun, for showing the interview he conducted with Hu Zhitao on December 9, 1966, in which Hu recounted what Bian said to her on the school sports ground on August 5. Interview with Wang Jingyao by the author, November 17, 2001.

18. What I write here is a combination of what I heard that day and the interviews I conducted in the summer of 2002 with my classmates who were present on that day. On that bloody day, please also see Wang Youqin, *Wenge Shounanzhe, Victims of the Cultural Revolution* (Hong Kong: Kaifang Zazhi chubanshe, 2004), Section B on Bian Zhongyun, pp.2–24.

19. Recently I learned that the very night Bian died, members from my school's Student/Teacher Representative Committee went to report the incident to a leader at the reorganized Beijing Municipal Communist Party Committee. The response of the leader was "si le jiu si le." This was what we heard the next day. Interview with Liu Jin by the author, August 20, 2002.

20. In the old days, if a person's name was crossed out with red ink, it meant that the person was about to be executed.

21. Police statistics reveal that violent death peaked in Beijing in the short period between August 20 and the end of September, during which 1772 people were beaten to death.

22. Deng Tuo was a member of the "Three-Family Village" that was denounced in the spring of 1966 as one of the first targets of the Cultural Revolution. *Yanshan Yehua* [*Evening Talk by Mountain Yan*], a collection of his essays written mostly in the early 1960s, was severely criticized at this time. Many essays became known because of the public denouncement of the book.

23. Qincheng Prison gained a notorious reputation during the Cultural Revolution for its mistreatment of inmates there, many of whom were former ranking communist officials and important intellectuals imprisoned for alleged high political crimes.

24. The reason for both my uncles' imprisonment at Qincheng had to do with a case that involved, among other people, John Leighton Stuart, one time president of Yanjing (Yenching) University and the ambassador of the United States to China prior to the founding of the PRC. For details of the case, how my third uncle Ye Duyi survived the Qincheng Prison and his other experiences during the Cultural Revolution, please see Ye Duyi, *Sui jiusi qi you wei hui* [*I Have No Regret Even If I Had to Die Nine Times*] (Beijing: Beijing Shiyue wenyi chubanshe, 1999).

25. The term was used during the Cultural Revolution to describe the hair that was half shaved. This was a way to humiliate those politically black people.

26. Central Cultural Revolution Small Group was established at the beginning of the Cultural Revolution to lead the political movement. It became extremely powerful over time.

27. Stefan Zweig (1881–1942), an Austrian writer.

28. Roman Rolland (1866–1944), French writer, musician and social activist.

29. I don't have insider's information about the lively and rather bizarre youth activities. For an insider's perspective, see Luhan, "Pai bozi yu eigeer" ("Dating and Hegel"), *Qiaobao*, B16, May 25, 2003.

30. A dossier contained information about a person's family background, personal and political history, appraisals of the person's performation in political movements by the party organization, and so forth. The content of a dossier was not supposed to be revealed to the concerned individual. Dossiers were kept by the personnel department in a work unit.

Chapter Four   Up to the Mountains, Down to the Countryside

1. A total of 17 million urban youth across China were sent down to the countryside between 1962 and the end of the 1970s. The total number of students in our age group was 4 million. The majority went to the countryside or state farms.
2. Ray Young's book *Spider Eaters* describes how hard it was for her to return to the city. See Chapter 23 of that book.
3. These lines are from Mao Zedong's poem "*Loushan Guan*" ("The Loushan Pass"), see *Poems of Mao Zedong*, translated by Gu Zhengkun (Beijing: Peking University Press, 1993), p.75.
4. These were Mao's words.
5. There were very few art products available during the Cultural Revolution. What dominated the cultural scene were the so-called eight model plays. Jiang Qing was personally involved in the production of these plays.
6. The incident took place on September 13, 1971, when the airplane carrying Lin Biao and his family crashed in Outer Mongolia. The party documents alleged that Lin Biao had attempted to assassinate Mao. When the scheme was discovered, Lin Biao panicked and fled with his family in a military Trident jet. Their intended destination was the Soviet Union. Up until the "September 13 Incident," Lin Biao's image in the public mind had been the most loyal follower of Chairman Mao. As a matter of fact, he had been declared Mao's chosen successor by the party in 1969. The news took everybody by surprise. Recently there have been books published in the West to challenge the allegations. See, for instance, Qiu Jin, *The Culture of Power: The Lin Biao Incident and the Cultural Revolution* (Stanford, CA: Stanford University Press, 1999).
7. See Lu Hsun (Lu Xun), *Selected Stories of Lu Hsun* (New York: W.W. Norton & Company, 1977, pp.25–33).
8. Barefoot doctors appeared during the Cultural Revolution as a short-cut way to address the severe shortage of medical care in rural China. As peasants themselves, these people usually were given short-term medical training and they were supposed to continue their agricultural labor while providing medical service on the side, hence "barefoot."
9. As a matter of fact, the villagers had been invited by the court to offer their opinions on the case before the sentences were decided—a practice called "mass participation in the proletarian dictatorship" during the Cultural Revolution. The overwhelming opinion among the villagers was that the man's life should be spared. Allegedly it was the woman's idea to kill her husband and the young man was simply tricked into the scheme. The villagers' view was apparently not heeded by the court.
10. This festival is the second important traditional festival for the Chinese people. This is usually an occasion for family reunion. The first important festival is the Chinese lunar New Year.
11. Many government employees were sent to "cadres' schools" to do manual labor around this time.

Chapter Five   Worker–Peasant–Soldier Students

1. Between 1971 and 1976 Chinese universities and colleges enrolled a total of 940,000 worker–peasant–soldier students upon a "recommendation system." In 1973, the year we both went to college, an examination had been held to test the candidates' academic level. The results of the examination soon became invalid after a protest by Zhang Tiesheng, a young man from Liaoning province, who turned in a blank examination paper. The attempted resumption of the examination system was thereafter criticized as evidence of a revival of bourgeois educational line. No more examinations were held in the following years.
2. The campaign's ostensible target was Confucius. But the real target was Zhou Enlai.
3. Pu Songling lived in the seventeenth century and was the author of many ghost stories that are collected in *Pu Songling Ji* [*Collected Works of Pu Songling*] (Shanghai: Zhonghua Shujue, 1962).
4. Qingming festival is a traditional festival when the Chinese pay homage to the dead.

Afterword

1. Some book that have dealt with the subject include Xu Youyu ed., *1966: Wumen Nayidai de Huiyi* [*1966: The Reminiscences of Our Generation*] (Beijing: Zhongguo wenlian chubanshe, 1998); Yu Kaiwei ed. *Chanhui haishi bu chanhui* [*Repentant or Not Repentant*] (Beijing: Zhongguo gongren chubanshe, 2004).
2. Please see Liu Xiaomeng, *Zhongguo zhiqing koushu shi* [*Oral History of Chinese Educated Youth*] (Beijing: Zhongguo shehui kexue chubanshe, 2004), Introduction; Chen Yixin, "Cong xiafang dao xiagang" ("From Sent-down to Laid Off"), *Twentieth-first Century*, 56, December 1999, pp.122–135; Vanessa lau, "Forgotten Generation," *Dollars & Sense*, 228, March / April 2000, pp.10–13, p.39. Among Western scholars' works on the "Up to the Mountains & Down to the Countryside" movement, please see Thomas Berns-Stein, *Up to the Mountains and Down to the Villages: The Transfer of Youth from Urban to Rural China* (New Haven, CT: Yale University Press, 1977).
3. In both cases, there was a lapse between betrothal and marriage. The usual marriage age in the locality is in the late teens and early twenties.
4. See Francis Fukuyawa, *The End of History and the Last Man*.
5. *Shanghai Baobei* [*Shanghai Baby*] is the title of a popular novel written by Wei Hui. The book has been translated into English by the Washington Square Press, in New York, NY, in 2002.

Index

135, 148; beginnings of, 5, 67–8, 69,
72–3, 74; "bystanders" during, 71, 94; as
creating a generation, 2;
criticizing/challenging of, 10, 71, 121,
136; daily life during, 5–6; and decline in
political usefulness of students, 97;
exposing during, 59, 72; "high tide" of,
70; last years of, 94, 111, 129, 136; legacy
of, 139, 148; lessons learned from, 96,
143; and Mao, 2, 69, 70, 73, 75, 76, 77,
80–81; memoirs about, 5; mistakes
during, 90; paradoxes of, 6, 92, 95; "red
terror" month (August 1966) of, 5–6, 18,
69, 76–84, 148–50; resentment against,
121; and "revolutionizing the students"
movement, 4, 52, 69; as sensitive topic, 3;
silence about, 149; suspension of classes
during, 72; targets during, 71, 72, 73–4,
77, 79, 85, 91, 94, 95; violence during,
2–4, 7, 69, 76–84, 88–91, 148–50; Ye
Weili concerns about, 82, 96, 127, 139.
See also specific person or topic
Cultural Revolution Committee, 78
"cure the illness and save the patient" (Mao
quotation), 77

dancing: Ma Xiaodong's interest in, 40
Darwin, Charles, 50
dating, 95. *See also* love; romance
Dayuan. See compounds
December 9th, 1935, Student Movement,
12, 13
delinquency, 35
Democratic League, 47
Deng Tuo, 70, 84
Deng Xiaoping, 71, 73, 129, 132, 136
detective stories, 65
diaries: of children, 60–1
diary, Ye Weili's, 84, 127
discrimination, 42, 47–50, 55, 73–4, 75–6,
131
"The Dismissal of Hai Rui from Office"
(Yao Wenyuan), 69, 72
divorce, 18–19
domestic helpers, 31–2
dossiers, 96, 127
drawings/pictures: confiscation of Ye Weili's
nude, 67, 84
Du Fu, 43

Dulles, John Foster, 51, 54, 56
Dumas, Alexandre, 121

"Early Spring" (film), 65
"eating bitterness," 57
economic reform, 137
educated youth. See *zhiqing*
educational system, 64–5, 73, 97, 129–30,
132, 142. *See also* college(s); elementary
schools; schools; secondary schools
eighteenth birthdays, 94, 99
elementary schools, 23, 37–44, 63, 138, 139
embezzlement, 124–5, 135
"enemy broadcasts," 122
Engels, Friedrich, 108
English: Wang as teacher of, 53; Ye Weili as
teacher of, 132, 138–40; Ye Weili's uncle
as tutor of, 86; *zhinging* decisions to
study, 122
English class: incident in Ye Weili's, 131
entrance examinations, 38, 41, 52, 72, 73,
129
etiquette, 37, 49. *See also* rudeness
European literature, 121
everyday life, 5–6
excellence: striving for, 38–9
exposing: during Cultural Revolution, 56–7,
59, 72
extracurricular activities, 56
extramarital affairs, 118. *See also* concubines

fairy tales, 24, 25, 26, 65
fame/recognition: seeking for, 65
family background: during Cultural
Revolution, 73, 81, 82; and friendships,
54; and Red Guards, 81; and
"revolutionizing the students" movement,
54–5
family life: and domestic helpers, 31–2; and
famine years, 44–7; importance of, 23; of
Ma Xiaodong, 27–32, 44–6, 88; of Ye
Weili's, 27, 29–32, 45–7, 87
famine, 10, 44–7, 93, 102
Fan Lili, 44–5, 54, 102
father, of Ma Xiaodong: and beating of wife
by Red Guards, 7, 88, 89, 90, 149;
childhood and youth of, 19–20; and
communist revolution, 10, 20;
disciplining of children by, 29; during

Printed in the United States
76680LV00003B/73

9 781403 969965